To Sally!
My new friend in
Washington (N.C.)!
Brad Stuey

To Amanda (walking)
and Anne!
Best wishes!
Brad.

Coast to Coast

A Prisoner *of*
My Own Dream

Brad Storey

Editing, layout and design by George Reed

Cover photos and portrait on page 6 by Faith Baker

Maps and interior photos by Brad Storey

"Taking the dog out for a long, long walk" © 2012 Casa Grande Valley Newspapers Inc., used by permission.

ISBN-13: 978-1490591780
ISBN-10: 1490591788

This book is dedicated to my six grandchildren: Jackson, Nicolas, Avery, Mitchel, Scarlett, and Hugo; and to my seven great-nephews and great-nieces: Sam, Conor, Erin, Mark, Michaela, Kayte, and Kade. I just wanted them to know.

And to my sister, June, who, when I was worried about my first role on stage, told me, "You don't have to be nervous. They're gonna love it!" And she was right. They did!

Acknowledgments

I could not have made the walk without Xena, my Siberian husky. I could not have communicated with the world while I was walking without the loving support and daily efforts of my daughter, Lucy. She was with me the entire way. After the walk, she also gave me a laptop and showed me how to use it in writing this book! My son Isaac was always available and spent great effort finding me about a dozen places to stay and also looking up road information when I was in desperate need of such. My son Brad fixed my cart in New Mexico when I needed it most. My son Emmett gave me great support during the walk and afterwards while writing about it. My sister-in-law Jean Lewis transmitted all my blog messages to Lucy.

My nieces Allison and Sharon provided encouragement, caution and advice before and during the walk. (Sharon's words: "If you're gonna do it—JUST GET READY AND DO IT!") My niece Becca and nephew Nathan took me in half-way on the walk and then got me going for the second half. Their four kids are wonderful.

My nephew Rob, Allison's husband, offered great advice and gave me the place to stay in Alabama before the walk and again afterwards to write all this in blissful seclusion. My former wives, Margaret and Susan, have been sources of strength throughout my life and continued as such, before, during and after the walk.

I want to thank Lucy, Emmett, Tracey Kahn, George Reed, Pat Johnson, Joe Mackenzie, Beth Beckel, and Gary and Ila Alexander for being good friends and for reviewing this book before publication. Their comments have been invaluable. George also worked diligently on the proofreading, editing, layout and design of this book.

I want also to acknowledge all those people I met on the walk who brought laughter and warmth to my lonely days. I would walk away from them refreshed and full of wonder at the expressions of love they had shown. And lastly, besides those I actually met, thanks to all those drivers coming toward me on the road who moved over, if possible, giving me a little extra room. By doing that, they were showing their willingness to share their world, just for that moment, with another human being. I waved to every one of them and mouthed the words, "Thank You!"

Brad Storey
Mena, Arkansas
June 16, 2013

Contents

One of these days,
I'm gonna sit down
and write a long letter
to all the good friends I have known.
~ Neil Young

This is that letter
and you are the friends.

First Foreword

I first wrote this book in the summer of 2012, immediately after completing my walk. In September, I had my daughter, Lucy, read what I had written, whereupon she suggested that I write more. I didn't know what more I could write but I decided she was probably right so I attempted during the months of December and January (by now it's 2013) to make the book longer and therefore, I suppose, a more typical book length. What I've added still doesn't make it very long.

In the interest of brevity, I've tried to keep it short enough that the average reader, if there are any left out there, could complete the entire book within the span of seven months, which coincidentally is the length of time I spent on the walk.

It occurs to me now that the book would probably best be read, again by the average reader, while walking 10 to 20 miles per day, preferably in one continuous direction rather than returning home each day. This would create a realistic back-drop for the book and an appreciation for the difficulty I found in writing it, which was far greater than the difficulty of the walk itself.

If you follow this plan of action, do be careful in reading while walking because of the dangers of traffic (always walk on the left side, facing traffic). I would suggest you take a dog with you, preferably a larger one that can keep up. Don't forget to take some supplies such as a warm sleeping bag, dog biscuits, reading glasses if needed, extra shoes...and...other stuff you will be glad you have with you. Seriously, I hope that this account might inspire you to walk or write or whatever, and to become a prisoner of your own dream, until you reach your own faraway ocean.

Foreword

Write about what you know, they say. I know this stuff. I lived it. This is how it happened to me and how I happened to it.

And what was this "it"? It was the endless mural that developed in front of me as I walked. It became a constantly changing collage of forms and sounds and smells. The linear experience of walking on a long trek is very different from our usual daily lives, which are mostly lived in circles of familiar patterns and people. On the road there is no looking back for reassurance. There is none there. There is only looking ahead, unraveling the sweet variety of life as it comes streaming toward you.

It was about two in the morning, September 9, 2011, when I woke up in my tent in Georgia, a wave of fear sliding into my consciousness. This was my third night out and although I felt safe where I was, I couldn't sleep. What was keeping me awake was fear of what was to come.

I had walked only five miles the first day, eight the second and to my amazement, I had walked 13 miles the third day. I was making progress, but in the middle of that third night, I knew that I was taking a big risk, putting myself out on the road in the daytime and who knows where at night, hoping each moment that I would not encounter "bad" people. I had already been asked what I would do when I met those kind. I didn't have a good answer for that question, and now I was losing sleep over it.

I realized that, first of all, I was facing many months of the unknown, and secondly there was no way I could quit just because I was afraid. This was going to be my own reality show, but with no cameras or script, no concocted competitions or conflicts, just whatever came my way.

I've never done a bungee jump, but I imagine that what I felt was just like that moment when one steps off the safe platform and finds oneself dropping into the void. I knew, there in my tent that third night, that I was going to have to "guts it out." There were too many people who knew that I was trying this and I didn't want to let them down or, maybe especially, let myself down by recoiling in fear and retreating. I was trapped. I had become a prisoner of my own dream and I was going to have to live that dream come what may.

Seven months later, I stepped into the Pacific Ocean. Xena and I had just walked across the United States, alone, except for each other. This is the story of that trip.

Preface

At the beginning of many of the chapters and occasionally in the middle, I've inserted quotes taken directly from the blog that I kept up while walking. They give an on-the-spot report of what I was feeling at that point.

I also have inserted sections that I call "Others Along the Way," lists and brief descriptions of other people I met who made a difference in my day. All the people mentioned, both in these lists and those in the main text, were so important that any account of my walk would be lacking without including them. Together, these people formed a "string of pearls" which gave my walk the human continuity that I needed so much. Their presence was like a guiding rope, stretched coast-to-coast, which was always there for me to grasp and with which I could steady myself whenever I needed.

I have taken the chance of including the actual names of these people. They were all kind to me. If I were to use fake names or just refer to "a man" or "a woman," so much of the essence of my encounters would be lost. I hope they will all be proud to see their names in print. I'm very proud to name them.

Mandatory Foreword!!
Please do not start at Chapter 1—this is important!

Please don't be looking for me to tell you what I learned about myself, or about America, or about other people. I could make up stuff about that but I won't. I will tell you what happened. It may seem like a series of anecdotes. That's pretty much what the walk was. A series of anecdotes which became like notes in a musical piece. Together they formed the symphony of my walk.

All that I really learned about myself was that I could walk across the United States. Maybe I learned that I was a little braver or crazier than I thought. I suppose also that Xena taught me that the walk was just a moment-to-moment experience, which, whether I was struggling or laughing, would become my life for seven months.

As for America, this nation is way too complex to try to understand it simply by doing what I did. I got glimpses of a lot of goodness in people. To a much smaller extent, I found some tinges of racism and intolerance mixed in here and there, but certainly no more than what is found overall.

If the telling of details becomes tedious to you, the reader, just remember that the trip itself was definitely tedious and repetitive. That was the nature of the struggle. The highlights about which I have written come nowhere near conveying the real difficulty I had, which was to keep on doing whatever I had to do until it was over.

If, in reading this, you get even a hint of that difficulty, I will have led you to the essence of my walk. You too will have walked the walk, albeit vicariously, with both Xena and me pulling at the leash.

The Author

PROLOGUE
A Life of Change

(I was encouraged by my friend Tracey Kahn to include a few pages near the beginning that describe my life, especially how it led up to the "risky" decision to attempt this walk. If that's of any interest to you, here it is.)

Blog entry August 21, 2011: *About a year or two ago, I decided to cut loose of most of my life and try something different. It's taken me those one or two years to get to the point where it's going to happen. ...I figure I've got enough left in me to walk another 3,000 miles in my life.*

As a kid, I wasn't exactly a big risk taker. I was my mom's only child so I had a pretty big protective shield over me. My parents wouldn't let me have a bike because we lived on a busy road. Moving to a more rural area when I was nine was the only way I ever got to be on two wheels.

My one real hobby wasn't too risky, but it opened my eyes to the world; I collected stamps. I learned the names of all the countries of the world, marveled at their strange alphabets, and began to wonder what it would be like to travel. My dad also collected stamps. He died when I was eleven and my mom raised me through high school. I was an avid Boy Scout, camping and hiking and achieving the rank of Eagle when I was sixteen. I liked Ike and Dick Nixon.

I went off to college thinking I wanted to be a lawyer. I quickly became bored with political science and switched majors. I had no particular career in mind. Before long, I started to explore the world a bit. My camping days with the Scouts were over but there was a different kind of exploration beginning to take place. I got a motorcycle. At parties I'd drink too much and act ridiculous. I met my first girlfriend. All very risky behavior!

After barely graduating from college, I worked in a mental hospital for four years. During that time, I met my first wife, Susan, and soon we were expecting a baby. In 1969, we went to Woodstock (three days of peace and music!) when she was seven months pregnant! Our son was born two months later. When he was two years old, we divorced.

I got married again and started having more kids; more risky behavior. At the age of 25, my life started to come together. I accidentally became a vegetarian. I was a regular big-time meat eater until I went on a diet to lose about 20 pounds. The diet included no meat products and after three months, I'd not only lost the weight, I'd also completely lost my taste for meat of any kind. I didn't know if being vegetarian was risky or not but I really had no choice.

Then came more adventure! In Philadelphia, my new wife, Margaret, and I encountered a group of spiritual hippies who were travelling around the country in a caravan of 50 school busses, all painted in psychedelic artwork. After our own honeymoon in Florida, Margaret and I caught up with these folks in the rural hills of Tennessee. They had established a large (500 people, 2,000 acres) non-sectarian spiritual community called "The Farm." Margaret and I lived there for over four years; all of our children were born there, delivered by the Farm's midwives. We joined that group's movement to save the world through love, hard work and respect for all life. We all smoked marijuana and liked it. My life had really started changing when I had been at Woodstock three years earlier, but now, in the early '70s, it was changing at a rapid rate. (Note: The Farm is still there in 2013!)

In 1976, we left The Farm to go out in the world and carry what we had learned there, into the general population. I began working as a housepainter and quickly became self-employed. It was riskier that way but if I worked at it, I made better money than working by the hour. With three kids, I had to work hard not only on the job, but in finding one job after another. I had to step up. My young family was depending on me. Margaret also took some risk. She became a midwife herself and over five years delivered a hundred babies.

We continued raising our kids, even homeschooling them for five years. In 1984, my mother became ill, so we moved in with her and spent four years taking care of her and undertaking the mammoth job of restoring her house to decent shape. My mom died in 1988 and I inherited the house that we had worked so hard on. We knew we wanted to sell the house and that's when Margaret suggested something unusual. Margaret said, "Let's take the kids and go to Europe." Our three kids were 16, 14 and 12 years old, two boys and their younger sister. The plan: Go to England, buy a small older camper from one of the many Australians who buy and sell campers there in a central London location (Margaret had done her homework), get some tents and sleeping bags and head off to France and wherever else in Europe we could drive to. That's what we did.

We travelled for exactly one year and visited 21 countries. We saw Stonehenge, the Riviera, the pope, Medjugorje in Yugoslavia, Athens and Jerusalem. We saw the pyramids and rode camels. We were camping out and buying groceries. We were spending less than when we lived in suburban Philadelphia. It was a perfect endeavor for a cheapskate like me. It was risky in some ways, but we were on an adventure.

After spending a month in Egypt with just backpacks (we hadn't been able to get permission to drive in Egypt, I forget why) we returned to Israel, camping on the beach on the Red Sea in the town of Eilat. The boys got jobs at a wind-surfing place helping newbies learn how to wind-surf. Margaret was tired from Egypt and just wanted to hang out on the beach. My 12-year-old daughter, Lucy, and I had more plans, however. We wanted to go to the country next-door to Israel: Jordan! The Arab country of Jordan and the non-Arab country of Israel aren't the best of friends. They had a barbed-wire barrier and guard towers along their border and no travel or even communication by phone was possible at that time. Lucy and I hatched a plan to take a bus back into Egypt and catch a boat to Aqaba, the Jordanian port right next to Eilat. We did just that, coming into the port of Aqaba not 500 yards from where Margaret and the boys were camping. As the boat came in, we could see their tent and camper!

The next part of our plan was to walk and hitchhike with our backpacks for a week or more up through Jordan. We spent 10 days there. We saw the rock-face building carved into the mountainside at Petra, enjoyed a hot waterfall farther north, ate falafels from street vendors and learned about Ramadan from the Jordanians and the Palestinians living in Jordan. We were able to cross back into Israel because of a weird agreement between the two countries that allowed for one-way travel at one point of entry.

We were fine and made our way, hitchhiking back down through Israel to our camp on the beach. My wife was glad to see us. To this day I can't explain why she didn't freak out completely at the idea that Lucy and I were leaving for another country, on the other side of barbed-wire barriers, with no means of communication. That we made it okay was one thing, but Margaret tolerating the idea? That was a miracle.

Leaving Israel we headed back through Cyprus and up into Turkey, Bulgaria, Romania, Hungary, Czechoslovakia and on up into East Germany. The East Germans told us that we were the first American family to drive through their country after the Berlin Wall had come down five months earlier. We chopped concrete pieces off that wall as souvenirs. A quick visit to Denmark and to Sweden where my wife's family was originally from, then down through Amsterdam and Belgium to France and back across the channel to England. The kids had decided after five years of home-schooling that they'd prefer to go back to the U.S. and go back to public school for their diplomas. I sort of wanted to keep travelling but I guess it was time. Margaret was ready to go home.

We sold the camper for next to nothing. (A man from Dublin bought it and *promised* he'd send the rest of the money to me. Right!) We flew home and enrolled the kids in a rural Pennsylvania high school. They did really well. Each one graduated! During this time, I got a job writing columns and news for a local newspaper. For two years, I took risks by writing about some controversial subjects and was mostly accepted by our readers. I even won some awards for best columns in Western Pennsylvania.

About that time, Margaret and I took the biggest risk of all. We divorced. She said she thought we'd both be happier. She was right. We've each grown a lot and we're still good friends, rejoicing in our children and grandchildren together.

I went to live in Arkansas and went back to painting. I was a Scout leader there also, making 15 years altogether doing that. Soon, however, I found a new love, becoming active in my community theater. My mom had been a professional actress and I guess it was right for me too, at least as an amateur. I got involved when I went in to audition for fun and maybe try a small role. The director gave me the lead role in a very serious full-length drama. I was hooked. Again, it was pretty risky business. I went on to do lots more roles and to direct seven plays for our theater. I wrote and directed a stage play from the original "Alice in Wonderland," and another one from the four gospels which I called "The Life of Christ." We had 90 people in that cast. Our very Christian community packed the theater.

In 2009, my Arkansas home town was struck by a tornado, killing and destroying. There was a half-mile wide, 10-mile long swath of devastation. The tornado missed my house by one block. It ruined many people's lives but the work generated by the destruction came at a time when the rest of Arkansas was in a recession. As a painter, I was busy.

For 10 years, a young man, Brandon Stockton, worked for me. He began when he was only seventeen. Brandon was everything in a person that you could love or, at the same time, you just couldn't tolerate. He was the best painter I ever met and was like a son to me. That summer of '09, I told him that I was thinking I might try to walk across the United States. After all, I was coming up on 65 and I had been painting a long time.

I wanted him to be ready if I tried the walk, because he'd have to find work on his own. He was okay with that.

The following March, on his way to work one morning, Brandon's motorcycle went off a long straight section of road and hit an embankment. He was killed instantly. He left behind a five-year-old son. I had never lost anyone so young who was so close to me.

In town, there were other changes. At our theater, there were several new people making some major changes. Also, my favorite pizza place hangout had to close. I knew if I was ever going to do the walk, all signs pointed to doing it right then.

From stamp collecting in the '50s to walking across the United States in 2011 and 2012—somehow there had been an emergence in me of a willingness to take a chance. Sometimes it was out of necessity, sometimes it was to follow Margaret's intuition, and sometimes it was to go to any lengths to put on a wonderful play at our theater.

If you've known me through my life as my daughter has, then I suppose it makes sense that I would try something like walking across America. Lucy told me that she knew I'd make it, and that I wouldn't quit unless I was actually stopped somehow. Her support was absolute. Lucy was more confident in me than I was in myself. I suppose that's good that I wasn't over-confident. After all, too much confidence would take all the fun out of risky behavior.

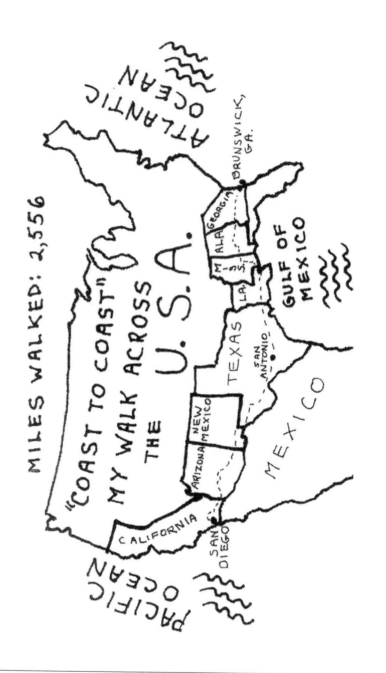

MILES WALKED: 2,556

"COAST TO COAST"
MY WALK ACROSS
THE U.S.A.

ATLANTIC OCEAN

BRUNSWICK, GA.

GEORGIA

ALA.

MISS.

LA.

GULF OF MEXICO

TEXAS

SAN ANTONIO

NEW MEXICO

ARIZONA

MEXICO

CALIFORNIA

SAN DIEGO

PACIFIC OCEAN

CHAPTER 1

Preparation
August 2011

Blog entry August 21: *I, of course, am not sure I can do this. I know I won't give up easy. The practice hikes have been reassuring and freaking me out at the same time. I've noticed on practice hikes, that walking really puts you in touch with the contours of the land. In cars we just go up or down and hardly notice except on extreme slopes. When walking, every rise is noticeably harder than walking downhill. Anyway, there's ups and downs. My theory is to enjoy the downhills and just DO the uphills. It's really just a giant roller coaster out there.*

I got ready the best I could. I couldn't predict everything about a walk like this, and that's actually a good thing. Figuring out things as you go is part of the beauty of pursuing any dream.

But I approached the whole idea the same as packing for a camping trip in the Scouts. I knew certain things I would need such as food, water, shelter, money, tent, backpack, sleeping bag, first-aid kit, sunscreen and so forth. Beyond those basic necessities, which I could add to or discard along the trip, there wasn't much in my pack. Immediately, I realized there was a limit to my list of equipment because I had to carry everything. I had decided to walk from east to west because I knew the West, with its long barren stretches, was going to be more of a challenge. By starting in the East, I'd be able to get some mileage under my belt before tackling the West. The only disadvantage to that, as I would later discover, is that winds, which are generally from the west, end up hitting a walker head-on. But all in all, the east-to-west decision was the right one for me.

I knew that physically this was going to be hard to do. As a housepainter all of my life, I had spent years on ladders, so my legs were pretty strong. My legs and my feet seemed ready enough to try this. What I didn't know was what kind of mental and emotional demands would be made upon me. For that, I couldn't prepare other than to trust that if I had to, I'd be able to grit my teeth, grin and bear it.

I spent the very hot month of August living alone at the empty home in Alabama that belongs to my nephew Rob, who's married to my niece Allison. They live in Washington, D.C., and were very happy to give me a place to stay to prepare for the walk.

It was good to be alone while preparing; the transition to the solitude of the walk was less abrupt that way. Rob's house is near Montgomery, right in the middle of southern Alabama. My only plan was to walk from the ocean, across about 400 miles of Georgia and eastern Alabama. After that first leg of my walk, I would return to Rob's house to rest. Making it back there, I'd be able to solve any problems and to restock. (That turned out to be just what I needed.)

During August, the extreme hot weather limited my practice hikes to early morning hours—dawn 'til about 8 AM. I carried my 25-pound practice pack each day for about two hours, five to six miles. I started out at about two miles a day, but quickly worked up. Xena had her pack and had gotten used to wearing it too. The name on her pack is "Outward Hound." Each day we walked, and when we returned, I weighed myself. I was hoping the practice walks were enough to lose some weight, but they weren't; it had only been a month.

I could have practiced more and more to really feel ready, but two things made me jump right in and start the walk. First, I knew I had to start in September. It would start to cool down and the beautiful fall weather shouldn't be wasted on practicing. I knew I'd be walking in the winter, but I'd prepare for that later as it came on. My second reason for starting right away was that I was tired of waiting. I felt like there was a whole TEAM of Siberian huskies pulling at the harness, and that all I had to do was say, "Go!" So I went.

I knew I couldn't take Xena on a bus or a train, so I had to get creative in finding a 400-mile ride. In town, I put up signs offering to pay someone to drive me to the ocean. A week went by before I finally met a minister who said his son might make the trip since he had relatives near Jacksonville. I ended up paying this young man to drive me to the Georgia coast, to Jekyll Island, not too far north of Jacksonville. The cost of this was a lot less than cab fare would have been!

I had 500 business cards made up and also had a sign made up for the back of my pack. It said, "COAST TO COAST FOR AUDUBON." I had decided to do the walk as a fundraiser for the National Audubon Society, a group that exists for the good of all wildlife, especially the birds. I've been a birder for about 30 years so it seemed reasonable to support such a group. Back in July in Washington, I had visited their headquarters. There I met their national public relations coordinator. She was all in favor of my idea and promised to help promote the effort through the society's many local chapters and professional offices. So I was set to advertise my walk by carrying the sign on my pack and by giving out cards so that people could follow my walk on the Internet and donate to Audubon if they so wished.

For Xena, I had a good retractable leash and a strong collar. I knew she would be on a leash day and night to keep her safe and keep us together. She seemed okay with that. I decided that Xena shouldn't have to pull a wagon or anything, even though she is a sled dog. After all she was not exactly volunteering for this walk. She'd been drafted.

I had all the light equipment I could carry, some food, dog food and water, and I assumed that my one pair of shoes would get me back to Rob's house. I'd buy new shoes as I restocked for the colder months.

That's about it. If I were to go into more detail, it would almost seem like I was well prepared. I wasn't. I suppose planning for this would have been like trying to prepare for your 100th birthday party when you're still only fifty.

And so there I found myself travelling east with this young man, Brian, the minister's son, to the Atlantic Ocean, to the surf along Jekyll Island on the Georgia coast. That had been the dream. That had been the fantasy, to start with one foot in the ocean, walk out and away from the water, knowing that the next ocean would be on the West Coast. As we drove east, I knew that part of the dream was about to come true. I was actually going to start. What would happen after that...? I really didn't know.

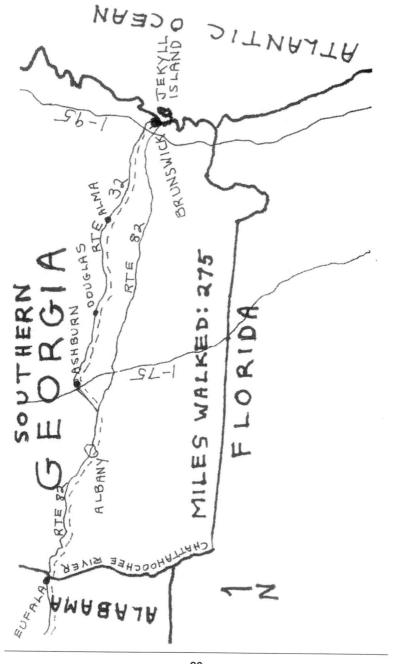

ATLANTIC OCEAN

SOUTHERN GEORGIA

JEKYLL ISLAND

I-95

BRUNSWICK

RTE ALMA 32

RTE 82

DOUGLAS

ASHBURN

I-75

FLORIDA

MILES WALKED: 275

ALBANY

RTE 82

CHATTAHOOCHEE RIVER

EUFALA

ALABAMA

N

CHAPTER 2

Georgia
September

Blog entry September 7: *First day out! I got a ride to Jekyll Island on the Georgia Coast, and have started my walk from the campground there. I have not gotten as far as I hope today. My shoulders are sore from a pack that is a little heavier than I had hoped. I am camped in the side yard of a church for the night and I hope my shoulders loosen up a little bit tomorrow and my feet aren't sore and I'm just keeping my fingers crossed at this point.*

When I first set out from Jekyll Island on the Georgia coast, I had high hopes but unsure expectations. With one foot in the Atlantic Ocean at the north end of that island, I knew that I was undertaking something that I really couldn't predict. Planning, however, is overrated. I was glad that I didn't know what to expect.

The first day out was terrible. I was off to a late start after talking to Lydia, a local birder, and walking around a bit on the north end of the island. It was only about six miles to get off the island and that day I only walked five. My feet were cramping, so I decided to hole up in the side yard of a church, behind some brick walls. There was an electric outlet to charge my phone and a water tap. I was comfortable but definitely freaked out at the hardship I'd had in only going five miles. I'd expected to walk at least 10 and make it to the mainland, but there I was, still on the island.

As I sat on an upturned bucket I had found, I saw a scorpion. I didn't know it then, but that was to be the only scorpion I'd see on the entire walk. Not that I didn't worry about them. I had done away with 18 of them back at Rob's house in Alabama. I was not looking forward to scorpions. Zipping my tent tightly every night became standard procedure. Camping there on the church property, I knew that technically I was trespassing, but I was pretty well hidden. I slept well.

The second day I made it to the mainland—eight miles—and camped under the end of a huge bridge. The third day I walked 13 miles and made it to the outskirts of Brunswick, gateway to whatever's west on Route 32.

Near the west end of Brunswick, it was getting to be late afternoon and I was still in a rather urban setting. I came upon a large church right on the road, with the pastor's house next door. I decided to ask if I could camp behind the church next to an old shed. No one was home at the pastor's house so I decided to sit down behind the church to figure out what to do. No more than five minutes later, a man drove up and asked what I was doing. He said he was from the church, so I asked him if I might put up my tent. He told me that everyone from the church was out of town and that he didn't have the authority to let me stay. He wasn't mean, just not very friendly. It was to be the chilliest reception I got from any church on the trip. I told him sure, I'd move on. He left.

Before I could get my pack back on, a sheriff's deputy drove up and questioned me. I gave him my identification. I was tired and a little unsure of myself, being only out three days. The deputy had been called, probably by the guy from the church, to check out a transient. After running my ID, the deputy was generous. He assured me that although I couldn't stay there at the church, it would be all right to check other places nearby.

That deputy was the first law officer that I had encountered, and he made all the difference to me. The church's rejection had stung me, but the deputy gave me half a smile. Within another quarter mile, I came to a small consignment store where I asked if I might put up my tent. To my great relief, the two men there, John and Eddie, said it would be fine to do so. I had been through my first rejection and now would try to just relax.

I've already described in the foreword the experience of that third night, worrying about the future of my walk. I was not going to quit. Leaving Brunswick the next morning with a new resolve, I headed out on that rural Route 32 and saw the long white line stretched before me.

I was quite unsure about even making it across Georgia. After all, it was almost 300 miles to Alabama, then another 100 or more back to Rob's. Having his house as my first real goal was a great idea. It made me stretch to walk that first 400 miles, but it also gave me a guaranteed place to rest, repack, or even reconsider. It would only be one-sixth of the whole distance, but I knew that if I made it that far, when I left there I would no longer be a rookie. At that point, I could begin to hope I might actually make it all the way.

But there I was, still in eastern Georgia. When I hadn't gone even 100 miles, I realized I'd made a serious mistake. Trying to keep the weight down in my pack, I hadn't brought an extra pair of shoes. A new pair on my feet might have lasted those first 400 miles but I had put my trust in a very comfortable but well-used pair of sneakers. The shoe mistake was about to become a serious shoe problem.

My shoes were still together as I came near the small town of Hortense. Along the road, a man standing by his pickup truck offered me some cold water. He was Charles Brown, a preacher, and he apologized, saying I had just missed his church supper. I said that was all right but could he suggest a place to camp for the night. He told me I could probably ask at the convenience store ahead, the only store in town.

The nice folks at the store accommodated me. I slept on the grass area along the road at the front of the store. Before I bunked down, I could see that my shoes were actually coming apart, soles from bodies. A little panicky, I duct-taped those shoes together and figured I'd have to keep doing that until I reached a town with a shoe store. It would probably be about 60 miles. I was worried, but what could I do? I went to bed.

The next morning I packed up, had my ice cream sandwich and cappuccino for breakfast, and was getting ready to walk, when I saw that same preacher out at the pumps gassing up his truck. I went over and thanked him for the suggestion of camping there at the store. After talking a few minutes, I turned and headed back toward my pack.

But suddenly I just turned around and went back to him. "Does your church have any kind of clothing ministry?" I asked him, showing him my sorry shoes. "No," he said, "not really." But then he asked me what size I wear. I told him 9½. He said he just happened to have an almost brand-new pair of size 9½ sneakers that he just couldn't get used to. He went home, got them and brought them back to me. They fit perfectly. I was stunned. I could hardly believe my good fortune. Those shoes lasted me the 350 miles back to Montgomery. I never neglected to have a spare pair again.

Just as a side note here, Mr. Brown had a friend standing there with us as we talked. He just listened and it wasn't until he finally spoke that I realized he was aware of what I was doing. He said only two sentences to me. "Don't look back. Just keep looking straight ahead, right down the road." That was probably the most profound advice I've ever received, walk or no walk.

Two days later I had only walked about six miles, and was far from any town, when I came to a small concrete bridge that crossed the Little Satilla River. I decided to set up camp under the bridge and spent the hot afternoon alternately cooling off in the creek, washing some socks and playing with Xena. I had carried my old shoes with me just in case the new ones didn't work. By then I had walked about 25 miles in the new shoes, so I decided I didn't need my old pair anymore. I left them there on top of the concrete beam under that bridge.

Someday I'm going to go back along that route. I'll be collecting memories and one of those memories that I collect just might be that old pair of white tennies out from under that bridge. Of course some shoeless fellow may have made off with them by then, but if I recover them, maybe I'll have them bronzed.

I walked through the little towns of Patterson and Rockingham to Alma where I had my first newspaper interview at the Alma Times. I went through Ocilla and finally crossed the first interstate, I-75, in the town of Ashburn. While I was doing my laundry, some helpful citizens let me know that in the 35-mile stretch to Leesburg, yes, there was a place called Doles. I had seen Doles on my map. What those guys told me was that

Doles consisted of a stop sign at an intersection. There was absolutely nothing else there.

I knew I couldn't carry food and water in my pack for that long a stretch. I was accustomed to about 15 to 18 miles between stores, so I made my first route change. I headed southwest to Sylvester, only 17 miles away. There I'd pick up the much larger Route 82 on which I knew there'd be more frequent stores.

I made it to the larger town of Albany. Near the west end I came upon the town water fountain where about 10 kids and a couple of mothers were playing in the pool around the fountain's base. The kids had some unusual names, like Turtle and Little Man, as well as Elizabeth and William and their moms, Amanda and Brianna. The kids were fascinated by Xena and by what we were doing. They had endless questions about what I ate, where I slept, and how far I walked each day. I cooled my feet and when I left, I felt strangely wonderful, knowing that those kids, who promised to follow my trip online, would always remember this encounter. That was a feeling which would be often repeated in the coming months. I wish I had taken their photos.

I'd had a good time in Albany, but when I camped at the west end of town, I had an experience which was almost enough to make me quit the walk. I was in a sandy area under some trees and well off the road. It had been a long day, hot and muggy, and I stopped a little earlier than usual.

I sat down and leaned against my pack for a while. I was doing a crossword puzzle and hadn't put up my tent yet because I could still be seen from the road in the daylight. Without much warning, rain drops, big plopping rain drops, wakened me from my word-puzzle trance.

Scrambling around, I quickly set up my tent and threw everything inside. I got in, zipped up, and started organizing my bedding. Despite being a little wet, I was okay. It was then that I discovered that I had thrown my pack in with me without noticing that it was crawling with ants.

The ants were those tiny brown "sugar" ants, but despite their size, they could certainly bite. I started smacking and smearing them, killing hundreds of them. It took an hour before I was done with them. I was hot and sweaty in the high humidity, and I was exhausted. I had been in a state of near panic for an hour. Ironically, the rain had stopped shortly after I had leaped into my tent.

Lying there completely miserable, I decided to call somebody. I called Margaret, my ex, and described the ordeal to her. I was trying to keep it together, and she helped. A compassionate response from her helped me calm down enough that I finally got some rest.

I became aware of county lines as I walked Georgia. Coming into a new county became the achievement of a milestone, as small as it might be. I needed some kind of benchmarks, I guess. I memorized all the counties in Georgia and passed the time reciting them out loud as I walked. I knew I couldn't do that all across America. Soon, my benchmarks would become state lines, not just county lines. I was looking forward to that!

Route 82 continues on past Albany to the small town of Dawson. There I had lunch at a Subway with a man named Mark Mitchell whose wife was an Audubon member. Apparently he called the local newspaper after I left him because, to my surprise, the editor of that paper stopped me and interviewed me right there on the road in town. During the interview, a woman came up and talked with me a little but was careful not to interrupt too much. She said goodbye and soon the interview was over and I was on my way. Later that afternoon, about six miles west, in the very small town of Graves, I was walking past a rural driveway when that same woman called to me. She offered me ice water and a place to sit, which I was very happy to accept.

The woman was Tracey Kahn. She and her husband, Guy, had moved to Georgia from New York City and were now Southerners by choice, just like me. Before I knew it, they had invited me in for supper and to my surprise, offered me a place to sleep. In a house. In a bed! No tent! I came to know both Tracey and Guy very well that night, learning about their children up in New York and their adjustments to rural life in Georgia. I slept soundly. In the morning, we had a great breakfast of eggs and grits. I would soon be on my way after retrieving Xena from the stall in their horse barn. It must have driven my dog crazy to sleep in one stall with horses in the next! Out on the road, Xena was drawn to horses, barking and pulling at the leash almost uncontrollably.

I stayed in touch with Tracey and Guy by phone throughout my walk. (After calling Lucy from the Pacific Ocean, I think Tracey was my next call.) Tracey had been the first person to take me in. She trusted a complete stranger in her home. Many more people hosted me but none were more open and friendly than she. It was a good omen and I recognized it as such. When I go back along my route, after I find those old sneakers under that bridge, I'll be passing through Graves and I imagine I'll spend another night with these special folks.

My good fortune was just beginning, I guess, because the next day, another woman saw my backpack sign and stopped along the road to talk. She introduced herself as Elise

Hitchcock. She was from Florida and was coming to visit her daughter in Eufaula, just across the Alabama border. Elise was genuinely intrigued by my mission for Audubon and promised to do what she could to promote my walk. No one else had yet seen such importance in what I was doing. She wished me well. I camped that night just east of Cuthbert.

The next morning, I was somewhat surprised to see Elise again. She had come out to find me on the road and offered to take me to the newspaper office in Eufaula. She had arranged an interview for me the next morning. I rode with her just across the bridge over the Chattahoochee River into Alabama. I had made it across Georgia! I guess she thought I deserved a good night's sleep, so she put me up in a motel in Eufaula. Elise was so enthusiastic and generous, even bringing me a large bag of treats for both me and Xena before saying goodbye that night. Twice in only a few days, I had been given a place to sleep other than in my tent. Things were looking up. Before I got to sleep that night, however, another woman was to get involved, and this time, I would have to think it over.

Others Along the Way
Georgia

-Elliot, Donny and Lydia the bird lady at the Jekyll Island Campground.
-Laura Smith at the pillars who gave me water.
-Allen, the first person on my walk who gave me money—and dog biscuits!

-And then there was Jane. After seeing me resting near a construction site, she caught up to me on the road to bring me a plate of food from her daughter's wedding rehearsal dinner. Prime rib, potatoes and some great greens and cornbread. I told her I was a vegetarian but that Xena would love the meat. She wished me well and drove off. Xena ate the prime rib and looked at me as if to ask, "Where has this been all my life?"

-Richard, driving the People's Victory Church bus who directed me to camp behind his church, and the pastor, Bro. Hugh Harrison.

-Bobby, who bought me a cappuccino at the convenience store.

-Shirley Flowers who, on a hot day, let me sit on her porch, gave me ice water and introduced me to her dogs, Oreo and Shorty, and to her granddaughter Mercedes.

-Priscilla and Misty at the Paige's store in Hortense.

-The secretary and deacon Ed Drawdy at the Patterson Baptist Church who let me camp on the church grounds.

-Ed Graham, recycling Christian literature, who gave me a bible tract which I still have.

-And then there was Annette, from the same church who brought me an entire home-cooked dinner in a take-out container. It was delicious.

-The nice ladies at the convenience store in Bristol who gave me free Hunt Bros. pizza.

-Beth at Joyce's store in Lacy who told me of her life. And Carl was there too.

-The boss and Teo who let me camp behind the Rockingham General Store.

-Elaine and Belinda, two very nice shopkeepers in Alma.

-The ladies at the Alma Times—my first interview!

-And then there was Eddie who called to me from his post at the drive-thru window at the KFC in Alma. He didn't know how much his warm interest in my walk raised my spirits.

-Chad and Candace at Roadrunner's gave me a big coke.

-Jason Carter, in charge at General Coffee State Park, who rented me a primitive campsite that I could afford. The blisters on my right foot were bad and I was limping.

-Mr. Dale who let me camp at his retreat called "Kids for Christ."

-Ashley at the store who told me about Mr. Dale.

-And then there was Mrs. Ernestine Lewis in Holt who answered the knock on her door when I needed water and a place to sit. On her front porch, she told me of her long life. I hope to visit her again.

-Glenn Lott who let me camp in his field.

-The crowd of guys outside the Ocilla K Store who were amazed and curious about this guy and his dog.

-Dusty Varney who interviewed me for the Ocilla Star.

-Sandy and Seth Filcher, along the road.

-Faye Vickers and Tony and Angie Cantrell from TLC Locksmith Service who gave me a great place to camp and brought me a veggie burger from Burger King.

-Johnnie, the lady who invited me to join her for breakfast at the restaurant in Irwinville.

-And then there was Delmar, who first invited me, and then Tim, Jerry and especially Buddy Ray at the Bethel Baptist Church who gave me a church supper, a place to take a bath and a protected place to camp on the back porch of the church on a very stormy night. True Samaritans.

-Gip at the Laundromat in Ashburn. Generous.

-Ed Caine, a wildlife biologist also at that Laundromat, also generous.

-The ladies working at the Piggly Wiggly in Ashburn. High spirits!

-Corey Morrow, met along the road, who played pro football for the Dallas Express. He stopped and we talked football and my walk. A defensive player waiting for his first interception!

-Lady and her daughter near Sylvester who came to the door and gave me ice water.

-Matt, the Blue Bell ice cream truck driver at the grocery in Sylvester. He gave me a pint of ice cream—chocolate!—and apologized for not having chocolate mint chip. I was hot and loved every spoonful.

-Justin at the BBQ west of Sylvester. I think he was the marine who told me that the marines say that dealing with pain is a case of mind over matter: "If you don't mind, it don't matter."

-An older couple with a roadside stand who gave me free soda and boiled peanuts. The man shared his philosophy and advice about what he saw as dangers in the next large town.

-Jessie at The Watering Hole, a young spirit.

-And then there was Bryan at the EMS station in Albany, who took the time to map out the best route for me in getting through that fairly big city. I was lucky to find him after realizing I couldn't walk on the bypass around town but that I'd have to go through it. It was my first city of any size. With his expert help I made it.

-The staff at Dr. Jimmy Lee's Oakland Veterinary Office who gave me dog food when I had run out.

-Melissa at the Sasser convenience store.

-The prison gang working along Route 82. Xena and I were an unusual sight for these folks, men and women in orange work uniforms. They were all somewhat friendly. The contrast between their restrictions and my freedom was obvious to all of us but that didn't seem to matter. One young man asking about my walk put this question to me: "Is it a thrill?" What an unusual way of putting it, I thought as I studied his face looking for sarcasm. There may have been a touch of it, but I told him that, yes it was a thrill but it was also a lot of struggle. We looked at each other and I think we struck a balance that felt right. We all wished each other well and with a wave and some smiles, we continued on our separate paths.

-Mark Mitchell at the Subway in Dawson. He bought me my sandwich and asked me to join him. His wife, he explained, is an Audubon member, active in the local chapter in Albany, 20 miles back. I realized that no one from the national office had told me that a chapter existed there. I began to wonder just what I'd have to do to not miss any other Audubon connections. As it turned out, there'd be no other chances until Mississippi.

-Tommy Roundtree who interviewed me for the Dawson newspaper.

-Jeff and Donna and their daughter Madison. Generous.

CHAPTER 3

Oases in the Wilderness of the Road

Before I tell about the disheveled woman in Eufaula, it's important to describe the main connection with reality that I found out there on the road—CONVENIENCE STORES! When walking the highways, even a poorly stocked, small-town or privately-owned store becomes a big deal. I started to have preferences for the big stores like Shell and Valero, and after a while thought of myself as sort of a convenience store connoisseur. I guess that's defined as someone who knows what they like, but in my case my standards weren't all that high. I was someone who was just so grateful to find any store along the road, as long as it was open and had people in it! Practically every store got my highest rating. I guess I wasn't really much of a connoisseur.

So I was always glad to see a convenience store, often from as much as a mile away. At that distance, I knew that in 20 minutes or less, I'd get a break. I never passed one up. Later in Mississippi, while driving around birding with Joe Johnson, my first Audubon host, I had a strong reaction as we would pass convenience stores. I couldn't believe we weren't stopping at every one! "There's another one! How can we be passing them up?" I wondered. By that time I had been struggling for almost two months, always just to make it to the next store.

At each stop, I would gratefully slip out of my pack, tie up Xena, go in and immediately purchase an ice cream sandwich. Every convenience store had come to look like a desert mirage, seeming unreal and promising needed relief. I couldn't pass up a store; even if there were two stores at one intersection, I'd go in both!

So these stores became oases in my Southern landscape desert. How literal that would become when I got out west I hadn't yet realized. A convenience store meant an excuse to quit, temporarily of course. But in the middle of a temporary break from any struggle, you can fool yourself for some moments into feeling that all that is behind you and all that is in the future are but parts of some dream. The only reality is the candy bar, the coke or cappuccino, today's newspaper with its news, sports and comics. Just put the dream on hold, man.

For an hour and a half, usually, I would sit down inside or outside. I would find a place to charge my cell phone, often outside at the ice machine plug, or sometimes inside, with permission, behind the store's counter. At least twice I forgot that I had left my cell phone plugged in and walked away down the road. Once I had gone a quarter mile! I'd quickly tie up Xena, drop my pack with her and race back to the store. Without my phone I would have been severely out of touch.

Each of these stores became my well-stocked market and rest area. I would carefully check out what they had so I could replenish my supplies with cheese crackers, sometimes even cheese, and drinks, either soda or V-8. I sometimes had to settle for a couple of pickled hard-boiled eggs from a big jar. Those eggs might be the only protein this vegetarian might find out there in the wilderness. Usually I'd sit along the side or back behind the store or at least lean against some outside wall, and just be normal, letting my mind rest as well as my body.

I'd pack away what I could, check the dog food level, munch whatever I wanted, and if I hadn't started with one, finish up with an ice cream sandwich. Then I was out the door.

Usually I had talked to the employees and/or customers about my walk. They were mostly very interested; most often they asked me what I was doing before I would mention it. Some folks would come out from behind the counter to go outside and meet Xena and maybe take a picture.

Some came out just to smoke and chat, but all who came out wished me well. I'm sure that in many cases, I was the most unusual occurrence that day in what could be a repetitive job. Whether the store people were very warm or just mildly interested, I'd come away with a recharged feeling ready for the next leg of the walk.

I'd slip my pack back on, untie Xena, and head down the road. But before I left any one store, I would always have asked about the next town. How far and does it have at least one convenience store? A Dollar General, too? Wow. Fat City, here I come!

Closed for renovations in Smut Eye, Alabama.

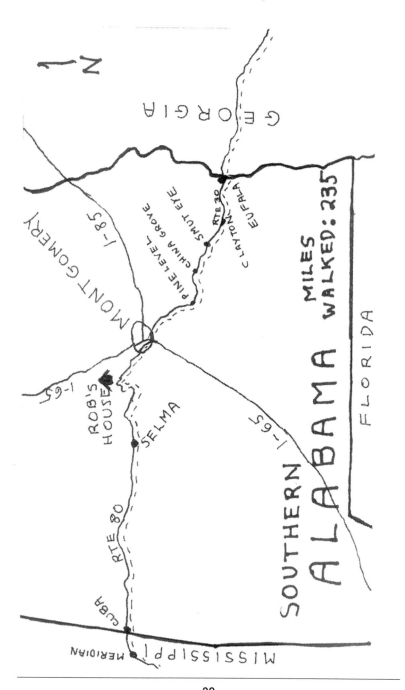

SOUTHERN
ALABAMA

MILES
WALKED: 235

CHAPTER 4

Alabama (Part I)
Early October

Blog entry October 1: *If she was acting it was pretty good acting. It didn't involve a whole lot of money. It was quite an experience. Anyway I'm off to Montgomery now. [It's only] 120 miles!*

Now at that motel in Eufala, I was looking forward to a second night in a real bed when, at about nine o'clock, a knock came on the door of my room.

A woman, looking slightly disheveled, began asking me for help. She said she needed money to pay for a room for herself and her two daughters, stranded by an auto mishap. The girls were supposedly at a McDonald's three miles away. There was an older man driving her around, helping her to find someone who could help her get the money. She said she needed 40 dollars.

I didn't know if she was telling the truth. I doubted it. The man could also have been lying as part of the scam, or else he might have also been duped. I first suggested that I ride with them to the McDonald's and see if there were really any "daughters," but I quickly realized that although that might smoke out the scam, I'd better just stay safely where I was.

So here's this lady claiming to be in need. I could tell her to go away or I could give her the 40 dollars. I had to give her the money. For one thing, Elise had just been very generous to me, a complete stranger, shelling out well over 40 bucks. But the most compelling reason for giving her the money, which I did, was that, if I didn't, I would never know. And I would always wonder if I had refused to help someone truly in need.

Giving her the money held the hope of finding out if she was on the level. I gave her an address to return the money, and she promised she would as soon as she could. I've never heard from her. She got some money from me. I don't regret it. You see, I really had no choice. I wish her well.

The next morning, I had a nice interview at the Eufaula paper and headed out of town. I hadn't gone far, still in the city limits, when I met a nice couple, Ben and Betty Spurlock. They saw me walking and stopped to talk. First they gave me 50 dollars (hmm!) and then asked if I needed anything! I told them that I hoped to find a place to buy some long underwear because, for the first time, that coming night in early October was supposed to be pretty cold. They drove me three miles to a store and paid for a set of long johns that I used throughout my walk, then drove me back to where I had been walking. Stuff like that started to really amaze me. I couldn't explain what was going on. Maybe it was because of Xena. After all, she was obviously an unusual and defining part of what we were. Without her, to many people, I might have seemed like just another transient.

With all the activity that day, I only made it by late afternoon to the northwest edge of town. I camped in the woods behind a Subway sandwich shop. In the morning, I went there and had my breakfast.

Whenever I would talk with store clerks, I would almost always mention my walk. Sometimes people were generous to me when they heard what I was doing, but my motivation was mostly to reach out to folks about the challenge I was undertaking. It could be inspirational and often provoked deep thought and great conversation. It also cured loneliness.

Also, sometimes people gave me advice. Some advice I heeded; *usually* I did. Some I ignored, but I always listened. In this case, the Subway lady suggested that I not walk the road I was planning to walk, as it would take me through a small town which had only a convenience store, but was such a hotbed of dangerous activity that her husband wouldn't even let her drive through it, just in case she were to break down. To help out, she called her husband, who drove to the store and gave me a ride five miles to the south end of town to pick up a different route west. I figured I'd be more comfortable taking that other road. Otherwise, I'd spend the next day and a half filled with anxiety, anticipating an upcoming bad scene.

I took their advice. I'd never know if that first route would've been a problem, but I was definitely more relaxed heading off into Alabama, my second state. Again, I really didn't have a choice.

I was beginning to learn to not regret the choices that I made. It wasn't until months later in the West that I had an epiphany about this. I realized I could consciously choose to not regret anything about my trip. Yes, I could have done more with and for Audubon. Yes, I could have written more as I walked and blogged more often. But I was overcome by emotion when I realized that my walk would be whatever it would be and that if I made it to the Pacific, the goal had been attained. Maybe regrets would be in order if I realized I had made a wrong choice which had caused me to fail, but if I made it, there was the proof! There'd be no cause for any regrets.

This understanding came as an enormous relief. I still had to make wise choices, but again there was no looking back. (Not long after that epiphany, my feet were in the Pacific surf.) But back to Alabama. At this point, I hadn't even made it back to Rob's house. I had many more choices to make and many more miles to walk.

Making it across the first half of Alabama was relatively uneventful. I was starting to do about 14 miles a day, maybe 16. I especially enjoyed walking through the "town" of Smut Eye. I asked one of the local ladies how the town got a name like "Smut Eye." She said that one of the original residents of that area was a blacksmith. He had come in one night covered with black horse-type dirt smeared all around his eyes. His wife decided that she'd start calling the little area Smut Eye in honor of that disgusting mess on her husband's face. Smut Eye's only intersection had just one old abandoned store, the Smut Eye Grocery. When I first saw the dilapidated building, I had to laugh at how dependent I'd already become on little rural stores. I certainly wished that this one hadn't gone out of business; I really could have used an ice cream sandwich. I fantasized about asking one of the locals what time the grocery would open.

It was in Alabama that I had the only fall of my trip. I was trying to walk through some high grass along the highway when my foot got hung up and down I went, hard on my left side, jamming the strap buckle from my pack into my ribs. For a while, I didn't know but that I might have broken a rib, but over the next week, the pain gradually went away. I had trouble sleeping for a few nights and struggled to breathe fully for days.

Fortunately, nothing was broken and this was the only injury I was to suffer on the walk.

After the small villages of Inverness, China Grove and Pine Level, I made my way into the south end of Montgomery, the state capital, an urban area for sure. Walking along the heavily-travelled east-west route called South Boulevard, I decided to sit down at a place of business, on a chair on their small porch in order to get a stone out of my shoe. Seeing me on the porch, the young man running the store came out and told me to get off the porch, saying my dog might scare customers away. He wasn't horrible but he wasn't nice. This was the first of only two times (other than the Arizona interstate) where I was asked to leave where I was sitting. (The other was a Wal-Mart outdoor shelter. There I was informed by a security guard that the small shelter was for employees only.) I started to leave the parking area but went back and gave the young man my card. He explained to me that too often, transients sat down on his property there and he had to chase them. He seemed to understand that I was on a different quest, but it didn't matter much to him.

I walked on and was lucky to find a motel that night that would allow dogs. Many do not. I was lucky because I was in a city environment. It was late, I was tired and there was no place to hide. I don't know what I would have done but for that motel's acceptance of me.

Leaving Montgomery, I headed out Route 82 toward Rob's house. The first day I made about 15 miles, ending up camping in some dense bushes near a Subway store. The next day, I walked almost 20 miles, the most I had yet done. The first couple miles were just urban streets, then the last 18 miles were along the worst walking route I would encounter anywhere across the country. The problem was that the two-lane road had about a 15-inch paved area on either side of the road. Many roads have much wider paved berms, especially if they have a lot of traffic. Route 82 carries a good bit of traffic and with the grass growing high all along the side of the road, a walker has to choose between standing still in the grass until the traffic has quit or else try to keep walking through high grass. I'm sure the highway department knows that few people if any are going to try to walk these long rural stretches, so cutting the grass probably isn't their top priority. I trudged along, stopping and starting as cars and semis whizzed by not five feet away.

I made it back to Rob's, buoyed along that last day just by knowing I was almost "home." Despite heat, ants, shoe problems, blisters on my feet, sore shoulders and high grass, I would now be back to my van and some rest. I was not positive I would continue my walk, but I was pretty well committed.

On the west side of Montgomery, a man at some gas pumps had asked me what I was doing. When I told him, he got a puzzled look on his face and asked, not unkindly, "What are you trying to prove?" It was a stark and serious question. I told him I wasn't really trying to prove anything, that I just wanted to see if I could make it. In a sense, that was the same thing, but at that point on the road, it seemed there was a difference in me. My ego wasn't trying to prove anything. I just simply wanted to walk. And then, finally, there I was back at Rob's. I just wanted to sit down and rest and think it over. I knew that I would have to compare what I had just done and what I had yet to do. I had done all right, but the warm-up was over. I would repack and rest only as long as necessary. I was now under no illusion that it would be easy to continue.

While at Rob's, I took Xena to the vet's to check for heartworms. That test came back negative, but the blood work showed that she did have the Lyme disease virus. They recommended more tests but I didn't have time to wait a week for those results. I knew I would have to have the tests done along the road somewhere. Xena was not sick, in fact they said she'd be fine for a while at least. I knew I'd take care of it.

Others Along the Way
Alabama

-Devon, Tiffany and daughter Hannah who let me camp in their backyard.

-Bo Rowland of Clayton. Generous.

-Macey Wright, who chased me down after I'd passed her house to bring me two bottles of cold water.

-Michelle, on the road. Generous.

-Jordan, a young man in a pickup. Wanted a picture of me and Xena.

-Kayla, on the road. Generous. Forgot to give her my card.

-Lisa, Billy Woods, and Peggy at the Brooks store.

-Brandy and Stanley at the next convenience store.

-The Brooks family in front of their home in China Grove, who gave me a place to camp on their property.

-And then there were the two guys in a bright blue pickup truck coming toward me on the highway. They slowed down to about five miles an hour as they approached, the passenger reaching out to me with something. I thought it was probably a bible tract. "Here you go, bro!" he said as I willingly took it.

They resumed their speed and if they looked back, would have seen my mouth fall open as I realized that I had just been handed two $50 bills.

-Lisa Addison, along the road.

-Ethel, an older lady, who was having breakfast at a convenience store. She told me she'd never been more than 20 miles from there and didn't mind a bit. "I like it here," she said. "I don't have no interest in going anywhere else."

-The Kimballs, on the road, gave me water.

-Kevin Ellison, working in his utility truck.

-Ladies at the Chevron, Route 231.

-Mital and her father at the Budget Inn Motel in Montgomery. She loved Xena.

-Stephanie at Bargain World.

-Nice woman at the I-65 Shell.

-Beans, AKA "Frankenstein," at the Route 31 Citgo. Generous.

-Mike Asher at Subway near Prattville.

-Lisa, who offered me a ride (to which as always, I said, "No thanks, I'm walking").

-Mike Moore and his employees Shaggy and Ashley at Party Time Bar and Restaurant along Route 82. Mike called me in off the road as I walked only seven miles from Rob's house. I was there for an hour as he shared his life and trials with me.

-The ladies at "The Outpost" who made special food for me.

-The church folks at their hot dog fundraiser at Mr. Henderson's grocery. One mile from being "home."

CHAPTER 5

Alabama (Part II) 🖋 The Commitment
Late October

Blog entry October 18: *I'm still unsure about how far I'll be able to go but with 400 miles under my belt, I'm encouraged. The real challenge will be, if I get as far as East Texas, to decide how and where I'll cross West Texas, New Mexico, Arizona and Southern California. The distances out there between towns can be huge, check out Sanderson, Texas; it's a marathon. How much water will I need to walk that far? How many nights? Should I go further north and consider Colorado, even?*

Leaving Rob's meant I was setting out with an entirely new commitment. For the first time, I was now walking away from my van instead of walking toward it. That meant that now the goal was "somewhere else" not "back home." I remembered the little kid who first asked me, "What're you going to do when you get to California?" I told that kid that I hadn't really thought about that. It seemed so far away. Gradually that question took on more importance, but in western Alabama, I just felt that I was going farther and farther from the lifeboat that had been my nephew's house. For me it was like trying to swim to some shore, far past the horizon. I had given up my only safe haven.

After spending nine days at Rob's, I figured I was as prepared as I could be. I had gone into town and restocked, having bought a new pack, a warmer sleeping bag and two new pairs of shoes. Now I was taking the back roads, mostly dirt roads, down to where I'd pick up the highway going west to Selma, Alabama. For the next 10 days, I followed that road, Route 80, winding through numerous southwest Alabama towns including Marion Junction and the bigger burgs of Uniontown and Demopolis.

My camping technique was becoming routine. I began camping in the rural areas between towns, stopping only at the town stores for supplies and to rest but not staying overnight. My overnights were much better out along the road where there were no barking dogs, no loud music, and most important, no one at all who would know where I was. I liked it that way. Xena did her part too; she didn't bark at night, which was important to maintain secrecy. In the mornings, I'd always pack up quickly. As soon as I stepped out onto the road, I'd have this great feeling that I'd gotten through another night. I felt free again to enjoy and to suffer through another day of walking.

As I walked, I was reminded how I used to walk through the woods while birding and that I would think how much fun it would have been if I didn't have my van. I would have been able to just walk off the road a little ways and camp for the night, hiding out of sight from anyone. That fantasy certainly had come true on this walk! Hiding produced high levels of anxiety and a racing pulse, but it turned out to be actually a lot of fun. The hard part was finding good places. It was always a little shaky. When it came time to end the day, there was only a short time to choose a spot. But rural Alabama wasn't too rough. There are lots of trees and bushes along the road and long stretches with no fences or signs of any kind, so I was able to slip into many a nice little nest for the night.

It was in one of those "nests" along Route 80 where I went through some real fear because of the presence of a large pack of coyotes. I had tied Xena to a bush and, as I was getting into my tent, became aware of the howling and yipping that is so characteristic of these predators. I was familiar with coyotes, having lived and camped near their habitats many times, but I had always had my van or even my home to protect me. Here I was very much unprotected. I knew that coyotes would kill dogs, usually after luring them away from safety, and I wasn't sure that they might not kill a human also. I lay there in the tent listening, estimating that the pack numbered at least 15, and that they were only a few hundred yards away. I had only my penknife, my cell phone and some pepper spray for defense, and I had to laugh to myself at how ridiculous I would be, trying to defend myself from a marauding pack of feral canines! I phoned Margaret and my friend George, leaving messages asking if they might look up the dangers associated with coyotes. It wasn't until the following day that I got multiple messages from them assuring me that there was little actual danger of an attack. Chickens or small untethered dogs would be fair game, but Xena and I were probably safe. That night, however, I knew none of this, and only fell asleep after a long, anxious period, punctuated every few minutes by that infernal howling.

On another night I was awakened by something very large moving about near my tent. I had camped only about 25 feet from the road along a fence line. I could hear heavy rustling and heavy breathing. I listened for a while, then finally unzipped the tent and stuck my head out to look behind my tent. I saw several pairs of glowing eyes, not 10 feet from my tent. I freaked out a little but quickly realized that these eyes belonged to some curious cows who weren't used to a camper so close to their pasture. I had to laugh and will always remember the "night of the living cows."

After Demopolis, there is a 36-mile stretch before you come to Cuba, the last town in Alabama. There are no towns along this road except for the small village of Bellamy. My map indicated that Bellamy was maybe two miles south, not directly on Route 80. I knew that this meant it was going to be unlikely that I'd walk an extra four miles just to go to a store. I knew I'd have to camp somewhere and push on to Cuba the next day without the benefit of ice cream or cold drinks. I was expecting that the "T" intersection ahead, where the road from the south joined my road, would be just like so many rural intersections, having a stop sign and maybe a mileage sign saying something like "Nowhereville 3, Somewhereville 22."

So it was with some palpable glee that, from more than a half mile away, I began to see what looked like a store sign. Back in Demopolis, I had been told of a store in Bellamy, but I had assumed, like I said, that it was two miles out of my way. In a car, that's no problem, but when you're walking...

I came to the intersection and saw that the store was a general store and that it had camp-type trailers and homes behind it. I tied Xena up and went in. I was welcomed by the ladies behind the counter. This was a very down-home place, not some sterile convenience store. It's easy to feel at home in a place with wooden floors, with walls and ceilings that have been around for a while, and with people who sincerely smile.

I bought my ice cream sandwich and my diet soda and asked about camping somewhere nearby. The ladies referred me right away to the owner, Donna, who was in the back of the store. I told her what I was doing and what I needed. "Sure," she said, "we can let you put up a tent somewhere back behind the store, inside the fenced area with the campers." She then told me that I was the second person they'd seen recently doing this very thing—this walking across the country. I was amazed to hear that a young man named Anthony, in his 20s, had been through a few weeks earlier and he too had camped there. She said he had a website, "Anthony Walks Across America." He had headed west of course. It was cool knowing someone was out there ahead of me, but I knew I'd never catch up to a young man with a couple weeks head start. After all, I had this big lazy hound with me that I had to practically drag along, mile after mile. It's a good thing that this wasn't a race to get to the Pacific!

After a great, safe night's sleep, I started out early along my last stretch in Alabama. As soon as I could phone Lucy, I asked her to look up Anthony's website, to put a note on it with my phone number and a request to call me. I knew that having an "advance scout" heading west could turn out to be very helpful. There in Alabama, I had no idea how important this connection would actually become.

So Donna and her wonderful staff at the Bellamy store had now become part of that chain of people who, through their sincere interest and generosity, had blessed my life and my walk. Also they warned me about the road ahead. They told me there'd be road construction all the way to Cuba starting about two miles from their store.

They were right of course. I found myself soon walking, for 15 miles, along this two-lane road, now being expanded to four lanes. Route 80 would soon be just the west-bound part; a huge area along the south side was being cleared and graded for paving a twin highway for east-bounders. I was surrounded by gigantic earth-movers, dump trucks and giant burning piles of cleared brush and trees. The air was filled with smoke and the road was full of impatient drivers and construction vehicles. I had to navigate around detours and traffic cones and squeeze along narrow berms. I had to remain alert for changing traffic patterns and drivers crowding more than usual. At one point, I could see a dangerous stretch with no berm going up over a small hill. Fortunately there was a state trooper parked off the side. I asked him if I could walk away from the road through a wide construction area where there was no activity. He said, "Yeah, that would actually be a lot safer. Go ahead!" I somehow don't think he had to deal with too many pedestrian questions out there. At least not since Anthony had come through!

The construction lasted right up to the eastern side of the little town of Cuba, Alabama, which was itself just east of the Mississippi line. I had walked 18 miles that day. I knew I'd have to find a place to camp right there in town because it was almost dusk. Normally I would have camped earlier, but the construction area precluded any such possibility. Besides, I yearned again for some store-bought food.

On the outskirts of town, I came to a very well-kept little church camp. Most churches had been very accepting of me so far, so I decided to ask at the main house whether I might put up my tent somewhere. No one answered my knock so I went over to one of the cabins where I could hear a television playing. I knocked. The television went off and when still no one came to that door either, I headed on into town.

I came to a small grocery store which provided my daily ice cream sandwich. The owner was there. She told me that I could certainly camp down by the ball field, that no one would bother me there. That sounded great. I headed out of the store, but before I got past the gas pumps, an officer from the Cuba police force pulled up in the gravel and got out to talk to me. We had a pretty good conversation about what brought me to Cuba. It seemed like we respected each other pretty well. He did, however, give me the following warning: "You know, you don't need to be knockin' on people's doors." Now I don't think there's a law, state or local, that forbids knocking on a stranger's door, but I promised him I wouldn't be doing that again in Cuba, and he seemed satisfied. I told him where the store lady had told me to camp and he said that'd be fine.

I understood, looking back on it, that whoever called about me (probably the person in that cabin) was undoubtedly frightened, seeing some transient with a wolf in tow, knocking on their door. That was understandable.

Surely there come times when any of us might need to knock on a strange door. Any encounter could be dangerous, and anyone has the right to refuse to answer the door and even to call the police. In fact, the police might be the best resource for such a person needing help. But breakdowns or illness might cause a person to knock and ask for help. I knew that I had broken no law, but I now resolved to be a little more particular about exercising my rights and to first consider all my options. As a result of this experience, I came to rely almost entirely on meeting people face-to-face rather than probing the unknown behind some closed door. When you meet someone face-to-face, you're both much more in control of the situation. Gestures and facial expressions become part of a mutual effort to allay any fears; knocking on a strange door is like situational panhandling. There seems to be less anxiety when people meet in an open-air arena where there is no threat to home turf.

I was grateful to the folks in Cuba for a place to camp and for what I had just learned. As usual, the police had been fair and no harm had been done. The next morning it was only a short walk of only a few miles before I saw the sign saying "Mississippi State Line." Two states down, six to go!

Others Along the Way
Western Alabama

-Robin and Manu at the Autaugaville convenience store, gave me free snacks and came outside to take their picture with me and Xena.
-Brenda and Wendell Carter in Statesville.
-L Gerard Savage at the Selma Wal-Mart, interested in my trip.
-Wanda Swank of Selma, an animal lover.
-Marguerite Johnson, a spiritual conversation.
-Patsy of Selma, generous.
-Susannah Brown in Marion Junction.
-Nice folks at Michael's in Marion Junction.
-Dorothy's Cafe folks in Uniontown.
-James Smith, on the road, ice water and offered a place to stay.
-Wayne, on the road, with his dogs, gave me water.
-Mrs. Young at Young's Grocery in Cuba who told me where I could camp.

CHAPTER 6

"Surfing" on People's Couches

Blog entry (back before I knew about this "surfing") August 21: *My second real worry is finding a place each night. Many nights will be between state parks, state forests, national forests, etc. Many places are going to be in the midst of all privately owned property. I'm not sure how I'll navigate that each night. Play it by ear I guess.*

Shortly after starting my walk, I was talking on the phone with my son Isaac, who lives in New Mexico. As we discussed my needs along the road, particularly those needs of finding places to camp, Isaac's girlfriend, Amanda, chimed in from the background, "Your dad should check out couch-surfing."

It turns out there's this organization worldwide on the web known as "couch-surfers," which connects travelers with people who are willing to host them. Whether travelling by car, by bicycle, on foot or on pogo stick, a person can put out the word that they are seeking shelter in some particular town or area along their route. Potential hosts periodically check the list of those seeking "couches" in their area and then can check the profiles of those seekers to decide whether to make an offer. If the host decides to offer, he or she phones or emails the traveler and they arrange a time and date for a couch-surfing visit.

Everyone involved must build up references somehow, usually from previous couch-surfing experiences. With me being a cross-country walker raising money for the Audubon Society, my son was able to get me started out with a decent résumé and so was able to arrange my first "surf" in Gulfport, Mississippi. Bernie and Barbara Walker were my hosts. They picked me up on the main road and drove me to their nearby home. As I put my things up in the guest bedroom, I noticed the lava lamp and the unusual artwork throughout the house. I knew then that this would be a great stopover! We ate together, shared stories of our lives and laughed a lot. As I travelled on west from Gulfport, Barb and Bernie vouched for me on my web profile, which helped me to be accepted by many more hosts. I stayed in about 10 more couch-surfing homes as I went west, staying both with families and single persons. From Gulfport to El Centro, California, this program made a huge difference in my experience.

I stayed in the homes of a rocket scientist, a Lutheran minister, a gay couple, an ex-military guy, a working mom with teenagers, a rock-climbing active-duty army guy and several others. In the Texas chapter coming up, I'll go into more detail, but one of my hosts even allowed me to stay even though she wasn't going to be there. We never even met! That was hard to believe.

Couch-surfing is really an ideal which has become a reality. For me it's been a validation of my belief that people can cooperate and help each other out. There's no money exchanged and no credit system. You don't have to host in order to be hosted, but you're supposed to promise that if you ever have the ability to host, you will do so. But whether you're a host or a traveler, all you really need to do is to trust someone that you've already had a chance to evaluate through their profile. You meet them, get settled in, and then kick back and share with them the stories we all have. I know I'll be friends with some of the people I stayed with for a long time. All my couch-surfing hosts, along with those Audubon members who hosted me, will always be warmly remembered.

As you'll see in the coming chapters, several times my hosts saved me from rain or from difficult urban situations; they gave me a much-needed shower, a bed and usually a meal. Each experience left me so grateful for their genuine human kindness.

Thanks again to Isaac and Amanda, without whom this chapter would never have been written!

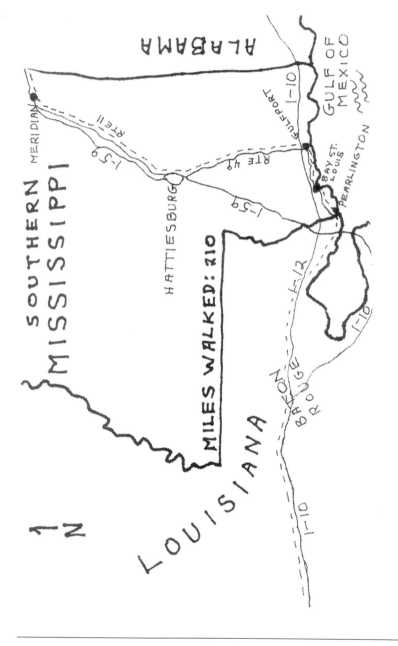

↑
N

SOUTHERN
MISSISSIPPI

MERIDIAN

RTE 11

I-59

HATTIESBURG

RTE 49

I-59

GULFPORT

I-10

BAY ST. LOUIS

PEARLINGTON

GULF OF MEXICO

MILES WALKED: 210

ALABAMA

I-12

BATON ROUGE

I-10

I-10

LOUISIANA

CHAPTER 7

Mississippi ✒ Audubon People!
October into November

Blog entry October 24: *Two things I have noticed as I come through the South. One is that many stores are closed, in both the towns and out in the middle of nowhere. Stores that used to be convenience stores, gas stations, mom and pop grocery stores, various businesses of many kinds are shuttered and in complete disrepair. I think it's ...I don't know. Has it always been this way in the South? Where many businesses are abandoned and don't get revitalized? I don't know, but right now it's depressing sometimes walking past places that you wish were open, to get a little bit of sustenance and there's nothing there anymore.*

Finally seeing that Mississippi state line sign was exciting. My third state seemed like a real milestone. I had only walked about 650 miles, but now I was starting to think in terms of hundreds of miles, not just how far it was to the next store.

I was heading for the small city of Meridian where I was to meet the first people from an Audubon chapter. I was to be hosted by Robin and Joe Johnson and maybe meet with the other chapter members. Joe picked me up along the road and took me to their home in the rural area outside Meridian. The next day, Joe drove me around to some great forested birding areas. It was fun to be in a car again and actually to just enjoy nature instead of struggling through it. We drove on dirt roads through national forest areas and around wooded ponds. Although we were especially looking for red-cockaded woodpeckers and didn't find any, we weren't disappointed in seeing only the usual gang of birds like the egrets, kingfishers, jays, wrens and sparrows.

Xena and I stayed with the Johnsons through the next day, which was very rainy. That night, we had a potluck dinner at their home, joined by eight of the Audubon chapter members. It was my first social fun of the trip, meeting new people, answering questions about my walk and learning about their Audubon activities like field trips and Christmas bird counts. The next day Joe fixed my inflatable mattress for me and then he and Robin put me on the road south to Hattiesburg where there was yet another Audubon chapter.

Hattiesburg members greeted me just like Meridian had. My new hosts were Larry and Linda Basden, who, like the Johnsons, gave me great food (a Thai restaurant!) and shelter, more birding by car, and we even watched the Alabama/LSU football game. I ended up staying with the Basdens for three nights.

The second evening they took me to their regular Audubon chapter meeting where I met the president of the chapter, a young man named Joshua Hodge. The next morning, Joshua drove me all over southern Mississippi. Our first stop was in the De Soto National Forest where Joshua had arranged for me to meet the ranger, Tate Thriffely.

Tate took us out into the fields within the forest where he could explain the ecology of those habitats to us. The first field was full of pitcher plants. These small plants catch small amounts of water in their pitcher-shaped flowers. The pools of water attract insects and trap them. Like a Venus flytrap, the carnivorous pitcher plant then consumes the insects by slowly absorbing them. It's a reversal of the usual pattern in which animals do the consuming of plants. Tate talked about the underground layers of earth and clay and how that substrata affected all life there. He shared the successes and difficulties that his staff has had in trying to re-forest the areas with hardwoods and naturally occurring pines rather than only the quick-growth pines favored by the timber companies. He described the legal issues and the cooperative efforts being made by the foresters, the timber companies and environmental groups such as Audubon and the Nature Conservancy. Tate is one of the workers who is out in the field daily, aware of the great challenges to the health of the environment. I was very impressed with his true expertise and his devotion to his work. I knew his time was valuable and I was honored that, because of my walk for Audubon, he made the effort to show Joshua and me his outdoor laboratory and share with us there his extensive knowledge.

That afternoon, Joshua also took me to meet Becky Stowe of the Mississippi Nature Conservancy. She showed us around the Conservancy's large tract and explained their mission of habitat and wildlife preservation.

That evening, Joshua took me all the way to the Gulf Coast, to the Audubon center at Moss Point where I met the director, Mark LaSalle. He gave me some idea of the efforts and the constant struggle involved in preserving a reasonable place for wildlife in a coastal habitat. The 2010 BP Deepwater Horizon oil spill in the Gulf (over 200 million gallons) and the general habitat destruction always taking place as civilization pushes its way into natural areas keep Mark and his staff focused on defending the Gulf area from Mobile to New Orleans.

Three times in one day I had met someone who was on the front line of the battle for the natural environment. Each of them was knowledgeable about their issues and tactful in how they worked for solutions. I was glad I had chosen Audubon to benefit from my walk. I began to see a much deeper layer of their work, well beyond the layers of amateur bird observation with which I had been mostly familiar.

That night in Ocean Springs, Joshua and I attended a presentation by ornithologist Bill Thompson, who, with the help of his young daughter, has recently completed a birding book for kids. It was there that I met Marsha Kazel who owns a birding supply store called "The Bird House." Marsha was kind enough to notify the Biloxi television station about my walk. By the time I returned to that area, after walking the 60 miles south from Hattiesburg, Steve Phillips, from television station WLOX-TV, was ready to interview me for the nightly news. Steve was genuinely interested in my trek; he created an inspiring feature for his audience. It was to be the only television coverage of my entire walk.

Sometimes along the road I would allow my mind to wander into fantasy. One fantasy was that I would be invited onto the David Letterman show where I would announce my list of the Top Ten Reasons for Making My Walk. The number one reason, of course, would have to be that I wanted the chance to appear on his show. Another reason would be more serious: to promote concern for our natural environment.

Leaving the Gulfport area, I began the 35-mile walk directly along the shore of the Gulf. It was inspiring just to see that salt water. Reaching the gulf was another real milestone for me.

The gentle waves reminded me of the Atlantic and caused me to think how far away was the Pacific. I knew I was as far south as I could get. Now I could only walk west.

As I walked into the coastal town of Bay St. Louis, I came upon a parade coming right toward me, with crowds lining the roadsides. There were lots of horses pulling wagons, which got Xena pretty excited. Apparently once a month the town opens up its streets and shops 'til late on a Saturday night and the town has a giant block party. The streets were lit up and alive with happy people; private homes had wine-tasting tables on the front lawn and good food was everywhere. My timing couldn't have been better. It was as if the party was for me! I certainly felt welcome in Bay St. Louis.

My Audubon connections put me in touch with Allison Henry, who came to meet me in town and took me for a birding tour of the area. We saw most of the local shorebirds, but I enjoyed the homemade soup she brought me more than anything!

Audubon also came through with a place for me to camp, but it was in a small parking place near a lively restaurant. I knew I wouldn't get much sleep there, so when I met a young man named Dillon, the conversation led to him inviting me to spend a night at the small house he shared with his roommate James. Sleeping inside that night was just what I needed so I said yes, absolutely.

Now Dillon turned out to be only 16 and James is 18 years old. How unusual for two young fellows to ask an old fogey like me to stay with them, but they were so friendly and interested in my trip that I decided not to question it. The two showed me around their small house which was absolutely covered with Christmas decorations, inside and out. They had put up more lights and greenery than most people ever do and it was still just early November! Here were two kids, basically making it on their own, creating the warmest and happiest little spot possible. Dillon and James and I walked around town with some other friends until about midnight, enjoying the crowds and the music. What a great break from my walk! I slept soundly.

The next morning I went to the Mockingbird Cafe where I had a great breakfast before heading west. I was now leaving behind the sandy beaches of the Gulf of Mexico and also would soon leave Mississippi. Some people in Mississippi had warned me about the people I would meet in Louisiana. "Don't make 'em mad!" they said. I planned on following that advice, but then that's good advice anywhere, right? As it turned out, I don't know which of the states treated me better. Through three states, I couldn't have had a much friendlier path than the one I'd taken.

From Bay St. Louis, it's more than a day's walk to the town of Pearlington, the last stop in Mississippi. I camped in a field of pine trees west of Waveland. In the morning I made it to a convenience store by a bridge. There I asked how much farther it was to Louisiana. They smiled and pointed to the bridge! I walked across the short bridge from Pearlington into rural Louisiana. It was a chilly damp day, threatening rain, but I was ecstatic.

Others Along the Way
Mississippi

-Jimmy Jordan, along the road, generous.

-Postmaster James Dillard in Toomsooba, interesting.

-And then there was the heavily-tattooed young family man in his front yard with his wife and kids who, after finding out that I was trying to walk to California even though I owned a van, asked me in disbelief, "Why the hell don't you drive?" I never forgot his question and never came up with a real good answer. He and I are from two different worlds, but at that moment our worlds met. There was no collateral damage, just smiles; I walked on.

-Danielle and DJ, a young couple who stopped to talk.

-The nice folks at Sam's Restaurant in Sanders.

-Ben Holloman at the Texaco in Laurel.

-The nice folks outside both the Shell station and Alfa Insurance in Ellisville.

-Cole Graham, a young man in Ellisville, good conversation, said he'd also like to do something like the walk.

-Claire English, from Audubon, who offered a place to stay.

-Patsy Yocum and friend who work at the Western Sizzlin' in Wiggins.

-Dee, who stopped along the road.

-Jerry Smith and Jack, who welcomed me to their fruit stand and gave me my first taste of satsumas, tangerine-like fruits.

-Wendy at the McHenry Stuckey's.

-Ms. Spencer and her kids at the Dollar General in Saucier.

-Don Foley, along the road.

-George and Donna Storrs, driving along the Gulf Coast road, stopped and gave me MRE's (Meals-Ready-To-Eat, military issue). I only took one (for concerns about weight) and finally ate it about 10 days later. It wasn't bad, should have eaten it sooner instead of carrying it!

-Chuck and Cherry Hall, generous.

-Allison and Muriel at the Mockingbird Cafe who offered a place to camp.

-Mark Madison and Jerry, had breakfast with me in Bay St. Louis and enjoyed hearing about my trip.

-Barney and Rose Cooper, stopped along the road.

-Shannon and Rafael, walked around with us on that Saturday night in Bay St. Louis.

-David and Michelle at the Wal-Mart.

-Vincent and Kay Caillouette, along the road.

-Robert, riding his bike cross-country to Ft. Lauderdale.

-Billy and friend, who stopped along the road to talk, then came back and made a donation!

-Sharon at the Pearlington convenience store, generous.

-The nice lady running that same store.

My typical view along a Southern highway
—the east end of a westbound hound.

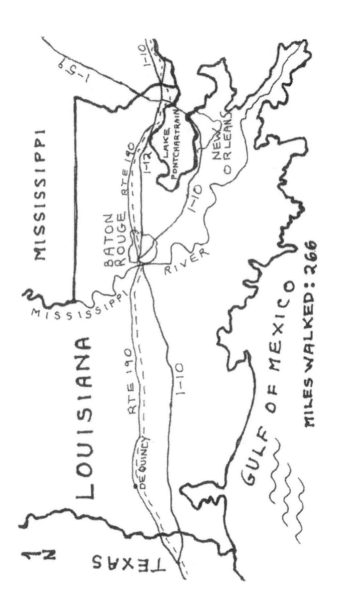

MILES WALKED: 266

CHAPTER 8

Louisiana
November and Early December

Blog entry December 4 (in western Louisiana): *The thing that I have noticed, walking along the roads, one thing, is that so many people follow so closely behind. I watch the traffic patterns a lot. And I've realized that a lot of people tailgate pretty seriously. It seems to be a really serious problem everywhere. Also as I walk, I notice a lot of white crosses with people's names, and dates along the road; people of all ages, people that I'm sure never expected to see their name on a marker along a highway.*

The first convenience store in Louisiana was a very down-home place with lots of unusual merchandise, like hardware and housewares and souvenirs as well as a hot food bar with red beans and rice. It was there I found just what I needed—a purple and yellow ball cap with the letters "LSU" across the front. For just eight dollars I could now become another wild LSU fan. In reality, I'm no particular fan of college ball, maybe a little bit for the Arkansas Razorbacks, but I knew it couldn't hurt to walk through this state showing the proper respect for the nation's top team (at that time). I wore that hat all the way across Louisiana. When I crossed into Texas of course, I took it off and mailed it home. I ended up rooting for both LSU and Alabama which was hard to do. All four states of the Deep South treated me very well, so I really couldn't play favorites.

But there I was, just starting out in Louisiana. I admit that I was a little nervous, given the state's reputation for being wary of outsiders. But I've been around long enough that I felt like I could stay on the good side of folks by being straightforward and friendly. Texas didn't worry me. I'd camped all over Texas. I remembered how I had been afraid, when I first went into Texas, that it would be a harsh law-and-order state. It was not! But Louisiana was an unknown for me. I had driven through before, but never really stopped and visited. And so, I donned my LSU ball cap and struck out into the "Sportsman's Paradise," the bayou country, the land of the Cajuns. The state bird is the pelican; it's even on their license plate! If I ran into trouble, I could always just tell anyone that I loved pelicans, and try to say it with my best neo-Southern drawl.

My first overnight in Louisiana was in Slidell, another Audubon connection. I was rescued again from a rainy day by Bill Newton, whose sister Marsha had helped me so much back in Mississippi. Bill took me on a tour of the surrounding area showing me the devastation that was still evident after Hurricane Katrina in 2005. Much of the edge of Lake Pontchartrain was still in ruins, broken piers and houses jutting out of the sand and water. Seeing it firsthand, even long after the event, was sad and profound. I was glad to get back to Bill's, escaping the rain and just getting some rest.

I stayed a second night in Slidell with a couch-surfing host, Charles Johnson. I didn't need the rest or the shelter, but I wanted to have a second experience on my couch-surfing résumé. Charles is an amazing young man, about 28 years old. The most amazing thing about him is that his job is designing and testing rocket engines for NASA. He told me he had worked at the Kennedy Space Center in Cape Canaveral,

Florida, and had recently been assigned to the John C. Stennis Space Center just back across the state line in Mississippi. He told me how, even as a child, he had been fascinated with aeronautics and rockets. Now here he was actually designing them, and seeing the results of his designs. He described how his work involved testing the rocket engines by strapping them securely to the ground, firing them and measuring the thrust they produced. Charles is a young man living his dream. And somehow, yet, he also would open his home to a traveler. There was nothing fancy about his apartment, just a mattress on the floor and nothing special for food. As he told me of his work, I realized that even though I was doing something unusual, my adventure would be for less than a year. Charles would most likely be living his dream throughout his life!

The next day I headed out to find the secondary road which runs west to Baton Rouge. This is Route 190. It parallels the interstate going west and was to be the road I'd take clear across to the Texas border. Going west out of Slidell, there's a beautiful shaded walking and biking trail that runs for some 20 miles; it lies just a few yards south of Route 190. Bill Newton had told me about this trail and how lovely it was. I started out on it and hadn't gone far when I noticed the "NO DOGS ALLOWED" signs. I really wanted to avoid the traffic on 190 if possible, so I decided to chance it. I soon found that there were officers in golf carts patrolling the walk, enforcing the rules. I had only gone about four miles when a rather stern patrolman, with very real-looking insignia on him and on his cart, persuaded me that it was in my best interest to "immediately" go out the closest access point and rejoin the main road. I guess canines can cause bike accidents and bite joggers. Dogs! Can't live with 'em, can't live without 'em.

I made my way west through Lacombe and camped in the woods near Fontainebleau State Park. As I walked the next day, I called the head of the Baton Rouge Audubon office, Melanie Driscoll, to ask about visiting with Audubon people in that area. At that time, she was 30 miles east of the city and offered to pick me up where I was and drive me west to her Audubon office right there in the state capital. I told her that sounded fine but I'd have to have a ride back to where she picked me up when we were done. She agreed and off we went. Reaching her office in the late afternoon, she and her staff and I had a long conversation about their efforts throughout the Mississippi delta and the Gulf Coast. The 2010 BP Deepwater Horizon oil spill impacted that coast dramatically, and (although the media has moved on to other stories) Melanie and her staff made it quite clear that the problem had not gone away by any means. Ecological impacts will be felt there for many years. Audubon has a strong coordinated effort of staff and volunteers working to clear damaged areas, restore wildlife habitat and prevent more damage. It is an uphill battle.

Melanie welcomed me to stay at her home and the next day even took me to a veterinarian's office where I was able to get a second opinion on Xena's positive test results of Lyme disease. A second test could confirm the Alabama test and they said they could call in a prescription for me wherever I was if their test was also positive. I knew that it was the only right thing to do for Xena. She was depending on me and I was depending on her.

The next morning, Melanie dropped me off back east of the city, near where she'd picked me up. I walked three more days and found myself again in Baton Rouge. There I stayed with another Audubon host, Phil Brown. Phil took me to dinner that night, where I had my first taste of genuine Louisiana red beans and rice. The next morning, Phil took me to the north end of Baton Rouge, a few miles east of the Mississippi River. I've driven across this wide expanse of river many times coming out of Arkansas, but obviously had never walked across it. Route 190 has a bridge spanning the river. It parallels the interstate bridge which is about five miles south.

I could hardly wait to reach the Mississippi, this special milestone. Crossing the Mississippi would mean so much more than crossing one of the big north-south interstates; the river is a true natural dividing line. I planned to take several pictures from out on the bridge. I ended up getting only one picture, from the very middle of the bridge. I had to take that picture through the side window of a police car. No, I hadn't been arrested, I was just being "escorted."

You see, as I was approaching the east end of the bridge, I began to realize that there were no walkways, nothing at all for pedestrians, only four lanes of traffic. The problem was very obvious, no gray area to consider. Before I could even begin to ponder my options, however, a sheriff's deputy called to me from his patrol car. I had no idea what he wanted but right away he told me, "Somebody called in and said there was a guy and a dog headed for the bridge, so I'm here to give you a ride across. Hop in!" In Xena and I went. We zipped across with no more fanfare for that mighty river crossing than one click of my camera. On the other side I thanked that deputy, grateful to him and whoever called me in for getting me past the impassable.

I was now past Baton Rouge and wouldn't see another big town until Beaumont, Texas, 200 miles away. I was well north of the gulf coast but Louisiana is very wet, even well inland.

Following the roads which paralleled the railroad, my camping spots became tougher to find. The state is full of bayous, and that meant there was standing water throughout the trees all along the road. Often I would find just enough room for my small tent and even then the ground directly under the tent was soft and squishy. The bayous were beautiful. Only a small boat could maneuver in many of these areas, and certainly there could be no foot traffic. In the bayous are great stands of cypress trees, their huge bases bulging out just above the water line and their offshoots, the cypress "knees," sticking up here and there in between the giant parent trees.

One of the problems that arose from the presence of all these bayous was that so much water created the need for many bridges. Some of these bridges had to be miles long, the bayou being that extensive. Now I suppose when you have to make a really long bridge you don't make it any much wider than absolutely necessary. This means that most of the rural Louisiana bridges are not only long but also have very little room to walk. Walking with a dog was dangerous to us and to the drivers going by. On the shorter bridges, a hundred yards long or so, I would speed up to almost a trot, eyes intent on oncoming traffic, keeping Xena on a tight short leash, but the longer bridges were not to be messed with.

I was told this very clearly by the nice folks at a convenience store east of Krotz Springs. After telling me about the bridge coming up, the lady at the store called the sheriff to come help me, which he did, driving me five miles across two bridges. It turns out they'll do this for anyone walking. They even escort bicyclists across for the same reason. The deputy's name was Ken Ortego. He was very kind and definitely got me past obvious danger.

On through little towns like Lawtell, Eunice, Basille, Kinder, Reeves and Ragley we walked. In Elton, a local policeman, Officer Firestone, stopped to talk to me as I walked the sidewalk. I asked if he wanted to see my ID. Smiling, he said he didn't need to check it. He said, "You've got a sign on your back, a flag on your pack and a dog. I know you're fine!" We talked for about 15 minutes, just standing there on the street.

By cell phone I heard from the Baton Rouge veterinarian that Xena's blood test had confirmed the Lyme disease. The vet offered to call in my prescription anywhere. Lucy was able to locate a vet office in the town of De Quincy. I would be able to pick up the antibiotics there and would have to give Xena her medicine for the next 28 days.

After leaving Baton Rouge, it had been 11 days of walking and 11 nights of soggy camping. I finally arrived in De Quincy; I camped behind what I thought was the veterinarian's office. I set up my tent in a six-foot wide space between the back of the building and a wooden fence bordering a neighbor's back yard. I was hiding there for the night, hoping no one would notice us. I tied Xena to one of the upright boards on the neighbor's fence; she seemed secure. I was trying to be as quiet as possible; I just got in the tent and lay down.

Lying in my tent, I was not yet asleep when Xena, seeing a squirrel or some other critter, took off at full speed, still tied to the fence board. Xena weighs about 50 pounds and was apparently more than a match for the board. It came loose and landed with a resounding crash right at the zippered door of my tent. I unzipped and clambered out to chase down my hound who was dragging that six-foot board loudly across the concrete. I caught up to her, brought her back and tied her up better. I leaned the board back over the empty space in the fence. I went back to bed.

I intended to get a hammer from the vet (they always have a hammer somewhere in every vet office, don't they? maybe for anesthesia?) so I could fix the board properly, but in the morning I realized the vet had moved to the other side of town. I left the neighbor's fence board sort of just hanging there. Next time I go through De Quincy I'll go back and have a little visit with that neighbor.

I walked back across town to the vet's office. They had Xena's medicine! They told me about the dosage and sold me some little tasty dog treats shaped like pockets in which to hide the pills. Thanks to Lucy and several veterinarians, I now felt that Xena would soon be rid of Lyme disease. We could continue the walk! I wouldn't have to worry. All Xena knew was that she was getting more treats!

It was 22 more miles to the Texas state line, one more night in the state of Louisiana. I had come in to Louisiana with concerns for how wild it could be there, but had found only warmth, help and LSU fans. In Texas, the landscape would soon start to dry out, but for a while it would still be cold and damp. I walked across a short cement bridge over the Sabine River right into the small town of Deweyville, Texas.

Others Along the Way
Louisiana

-Reggie at the Subway in Wal-Mart in Slidell.

-Daniel Parker, who sat and talked to me about his life in rural Louisiana at the Lacombe Bayou store.

-Dustin Renaud, Carla, David and Eric, all of the Baton Rouge Audubon staff, on the front lines of the work to preserve the environment.

-Tiffany at the grocery in Robert.

-Nice folks at the Piggly Wiggly in Hammond.

-Chuck, with his Yorkies in Hammond.

-Tara at the Albany Exxon, who gave me a sausage biscuit—shared with Xena!

-Joyce and granddaughter Delaney at the Wal-Mart in Hammond.

-Matt Stump, gave me cold water along Route 190.

-Nice lady at Louie's Quik Stop, west end of Mississippi River Bridge.

-Sherri—AN ANGEL!—who gave me a ride back to pick up something I'd left behind at the east end of the Mississippi River bridge, then back again to Louie's where she then made a donation! Thank you, thank you!

-Ann and Don Monk, a Thanksgiving dinner along the road!

-The Gonzalez family, planning a walk of their own from Louisiana to Tennessee. It was cold and they were heading north. I shared my thoughts.

-Anne at the Shell in Lottie.

-And then there was Mary, who stopped to see if I needed anything. She offered me her warm jacket, but I thought it would add too much weight when I wasn't wearing it. What a special person!

-Byron Miller and his wife, along the road.

-Joshua at the truck stop near Eunice.

-Mea at the photo booth in the Eunice Wal-Mart.

-Sandra and Stephanie, sisters, generous.

-The nice guy who stopped and asked, "Are you okay?"

-Yvette Tompkins, generous.

-Berlaine Boone, the mayor of Basille.

-Officer Firestone in Elton.

-Doug Rider in Elton who brought me a whole bunch of sweet potatoes which I couldn't carry. Wish I could've!

-Kimberly and Robert Apshire, a cold Coke.

-Tyson and Brandy at the Market Basket in Kinder.

-Tom Kersch at Thibodeaux's in Ragley.

-Kimberly, out on the road, generous.

-Nice staff girls at the Valero east of De Quincy.

-Amber and friend at the De Quincy Dollar General.

-Mary Ann at the Texaco in De Quincy.

-Kevin Jones also at that Texaco.

-Robert DeGelormo, who stopped, saying he was just checkin' to see if I needed anything.

-The competent and friendly staff at the veterinarian's office in De Quincy.

-The nice girls at the Dollar General in Stark.

-The roadwork guy in Stark.

CHAPTER 9

Regarding the Question of Guns

> Blog entry February 12 (in Texas): *The feeling of fear has two sides to it. On one side is anxiety, but the other side is that it keeps things interesting!*

Several times along the walk I was asked, "Are you carryin' a gun?" Every one of those asking the question felt that I was being foolish not to be armed. After all, I was alone out there on the road with only my dog. Those asking the question were always men and usually I told them no, I wasn't carrying. Once I said only, "No comment." These guys were men who couldn't imagine being defenseless in a world they know to be sometimes violent. I listened to them and realized they were truly concerned for my safety.

I carried a penknife, some pepper spray that my brother-in-law gave me, my cell phone and a whistle. I knew that these implements weren't going to do much if I encountered anyone who was bent on doing me harm. There were times I questioned the wisdom of being so defenseless.

Was it a wise decision to be unarmed? I could probably have handled a revolver pretty well. As a Scout and as a Scoutmaster I had been very good with a rifle, but there is a big difference between lying quietly in a prone position squeezing off rounds at a paper target, and firing a sidearm at a human adversary. I remember a few times on the walk when my fears rose up in me. At those times, I suppose I would have felt more able to make a statement on defense or, if necessary, on offense, by brandishing a weapon. For the most part, however, I held to my belief that the mind-set of *not* being armed was probably safer than the mind-set of carrying a gun.

Not having any weapon made me more vulnerable, no doubt, but it also made me rely on my positive attitude toward my surroundings. This attitude should not be discounted by those who see the protection of a firearm as the only real security. I made the trip without ever being threatened. I may have been lucky, but after all, I was walking to support the National Audubon Society not the National Rifle Association. I believe deeply in the beauty of nature, including that of human nature, not in the ugliness that's always found in armed conflict.

As a final note to this gun business, I always noticed the side arms carried by the police officers and by the border patrol agents along my walk. They certainly never had reason to draw their weapons around me, but I knew that in their line of work, those guns were necessary. I respect them for that.

Can't remember where this was taken!

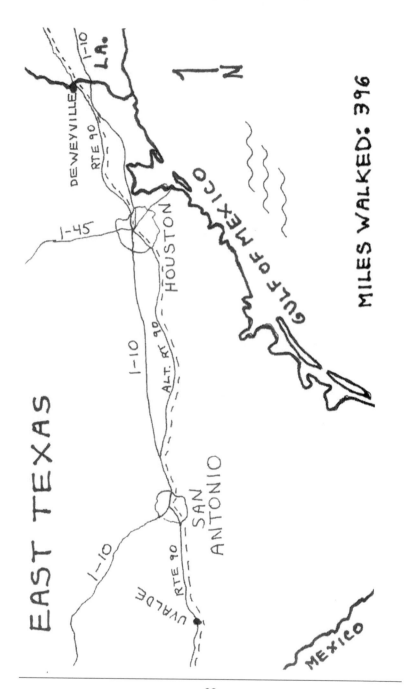

EAST TEXAS

DEWEYVILLE

RTE 90

I-10

LA.

I-45

HOUSTON

ALT. RT 90

I-10

GULF OF MEXICO

SAN ANTONIO

RTE 90

UVALDE

I-10

MEXICO

N

MILES WALKED: 396

CHAPTER 10

East Texas
December

Blog entry (Lucy's posting) December 7: *I talked to dad this morning. He was still in bed, sleeping in his tent in someone's shed. Apparently it is pretty cold. He has made it all the way to Texas, and plans on visiting my cousin and her family in the San Antonio area. It kind of dawned on me the other day, when I made the map, that dad is really like 1/3 or so the way across the USA. I mean wow. I had no idea it would go this fast!*

The first thing you come to at that crossing into Deweyville, Texas, is a Texas-shaped concrete monument about five feet high. It says: "TEXAS." A large road sign soon welcomes you and reminds you to "Drive Friendly—The Texas Way." As a driver I had entered Texas many times and I knew what the sign meant: "Move Over If You Can And Let People Behind You Get Around If They're Trying To Go Faster Than You Are." I guess that's too much to put on a welcoming sign so they just suggest that you "Drive Friendly."

The berms on the sides of most Texas roads are extra wide. People regularly move over onto these berms, especially in "no passing" zones. These maneuvers are sometimes happening in both directions at the same time, creating a four-lane highway where, only moments before, there had been only two lanes. It actually works out into a friendly roadway dance for the Texans and their participating visitors. This maneuver certainly relieves the stress of the passer but also does the same for the "passee." I mean who wants someone impatiently "pushing" you down the road?

I always drive the friendly way in Texas. I recommend it highly. As a pedestrian it wasn't a problem either, I suppose because few people would consider running over a man and his dog as being a friendly way to drive. Apparently as a walker I was given consideration.

I was now in my fifth state. Texas is a state so large that it made up a full third of my walk, over 800 miles from Deweyville to El Paso. I would spend most of the winter walking through this one state. I just hoped I would make it halfway through the state to San Antonio where I would visit my niece and her family. I've always loved Texas and looked forward to getting to know it on foot.

Right after the welcome sign was a convenience store. Two young men, Robert and Codie, both about 18, were hanging out back by the trees along the Sabine River. They turned out to be the friendliest welcoming committee I could want. Upon seeing my Audubon sign, Robert asked why I was walking for the Audubon. He thought the Audubon was the Autobahn, the high-speed superhighway in Germany. We laughed over that. I was beginning to realize that most young people today no longer recognize the name "Audubon" as having anything to do with nature. When I was growing up, people were much more aware of that famous name and of the relevance of the natural world to our daily lives. In fact, in the Boy Scouts, one requirement for becoming an Eagle Scout used to be the earning of the "bird study" merit badge! Can you imagine that today?

So after saying goodbye to Robert and Codie, I went on into the store for my ice cream sandwich and maybe some cheese crackers. It was quite late in the day. As I was coming out, I met another man who asked me if I needed anything. I told him straight out that really the only thing I needed was a place to camp. "Well, hop in," he said, and within 10 minutes I was setting up my tent within the walls of an enclosed wooden shed behind his house. It was windy and chilly and the little building gave just enough protection from the elements. I was really glad to be there.

My host's name was Chad. He introduced me to his wife, Amber, and their kids, Aaron and Felisitie. While we were talking, Felisitie went to the lemon tree in their yard and picked a large round lemon from it. I could see as she handed it to me that she was welcoming me to Texas in her own way. (Normally lemons aren't for eating, and days later, I still had that lemon in my pack. I decided to at least try it. It turned out to be sweet enough to eat like an orange. Apparently not all lemons are tart. I hadn't known that.) That lemon was one of the best gifts I got anywhere. Many other people gave me food and water, dog food, and even money, but that lemon, plucked fresh from their tree, was especially sweet!

The next morning the family gave me a great breakfast and a big bag of small treats and useful things like Band-Aids, towelettes and matches. I was getting ready for the road to Beaumont when their daughter came to me with a Christmas drawing she had made. It said, "All I want to say is 'Good Luck'." It was signed, "Your friend, Felisitie." I still have that drawing. Through my friend Marsha, at The Bird House back in Mississippi, I sent Felisitie a beginner's bird book. I believe

I'll have to stop in Deweyville again as I drive back along my route.

I walked on to Beaumont where I was hosted by yet another couch-surfer, a Lutheran minister named Sabine Lamar. She was preparing for Christmas. Over some excellent meals, we talked. She seemed glad to talk to someone about the daily trials in the life of a caring minister. While staying at Sabine's, an Audubon volunteer, Christine Sliva, came to take me out birding around the north Gulf Coast area. We went to Sabine Woods, a Texas Ornithological Society bird sanctuary which I had visited many times. Although we didn't see any barn owls, which Christine said should be there, I had a great time just being away from the daily walk. Breaks like this with another birder were always welcome, giving me the closer personal contact that was so often missing in the daily routine of my walk. Meeting people at a convenience store was terrific, but it rarely led to an in-depth conversation about environmental issues or (especially) the fun of bird watching.

At another wildlife area with Christine, Xena went out onto a pier on a small lake and, thinking that a thick layer of algae on the water was actually grass and dirt, walked off the end. I have never seen Xena go in water above her ankles so this was quite a surprise for her. She dog-paddled to shore. I don't know if she was humbled or not (it's hard to tell with dogs), but although soaking wet and covered with algae, she shook it off as though she "meant to do it." While riding back with Christine, Xena did something else I'd never seen before. From the back, she leaned forward between the seats and tucked her head tightly down next to Christine's right hip. Maybe she was hoping to stay with Christine and not have to do any more walking west! After another night at Sabine's, I headed off on the 75 miles to Houston.

After arriving in Houston, I was invited to visit the Audubon center to give a talk to a group of children at an Audubon workshop. Xena, as always, was a big hit. On a large map, I showed these budding naturalists where we had walked and where we still had to walk. I showed them my binoculars and explained that our walk was raising money for Audubon to help protect the very areas through which we were walking. The kids were a great audience and very enthusiastic.

Thanks to staff members Gina Donovan and, especially, Jessica Dubin, I learned that Houston Audubon, through the Aransas Project, has taken the state of Texas to court over water-usage issues. The diversion of water flowing toward the Gulf has been so extensive that not enough fresh water reaches the estuaries and bays around the Aransas National Wildlife Refuge. This area is the wintering ground for the whooping crane, a seriously endangered species which feeds on the crabs in the shallow coastal bays. A drop in incoming water to these areas has increased the salinity of the water, and the crab population has decreased dramatically. Bodies of emaciated cranes have been found on the tidal flats, and with only about 200 of these birds left, each death becomes significant. The Endangered Species Act requires that individuals and states are bound by law to not follow policies which create hazardous conditions for these species. The staff at Houston Audubon took the time to tell me of this legal challenge and I left there hoping that they would be successful.

In Houston I was welcomed by three separate hosts. Jackie and Ryan Carter, whom I had known in Arkansas, first took me in. It was the first time I had met anyone on the walk that I had known before. I had directed *Romeo and Juliet* back at our community theater, and Jackie had played the role of Juliet. It was great to see them and their toddler son, Jackson. Next, I called Elizabeth Lennon, a friend from Pennsylvania now living near Houston with her husband Michael. I stayed two nights with them, enjoying a warm place to sleep and a fun visit. And finally, a couch-surfing couple, Faerlee and Shawn Smith gave me not only a night's rest, but a tour of their section of Houston to see the most spectacular Christmas lights I've ever seen. In one large neighborhood, block after block had almost every home completely decked out with extensive lights and extraordinary decorations. Whole blocks had different themes and were in competition for prizes from the local community. Cars crept along through these neighborhoods, everyone in awe of the spectacle.

The next morning started with Shawn and me taking a 10-mile bike ride to a bike race. We returned home and had lunch. They then drove me to the west end of Houston where I picked up alternate Route 90. Now I had only 200 miles on that road to walk to get to San Antonio. As soon as I started walking, I saw a large brick sign, beautifully landscaped. It was about 30 feet long. Maybe it was the name of some huge housing development or something, but I had to take a picture of it. It said, "New Territory." I had to laugh. I knew that I was now heading on out into the real Texas countryside. It was cold at night, a little warmer in the day. I knew it would be that way all the way to my niece Becca's house.

Not far from Houston, in the mid-afternoon, I came to the town of Rosenberg. It was about to rain any minute so I didn't know whether to try to make it out of town, as usual, or to try to find a dry place in town. I was temporarily hunkered down at the town post office when my cell phone rang. It was another couch-surfing host, Steve McNulty. I hadn't known of any local couch-surf contacts, but my son Isaac had put out the word on the Internet and Steve responded. He drove 30 miles to come get me! Just as it started to really rain, we arrived at his home. We had dinner with his wife and kids and again I slept soundly, warm and dry. Steve drove me back to Rosenberg the next morning to pick up right where I had left off. He stayed in touch with me throughout the trek and followed my blog. We still talk and I hope to see him and his family again. Here was another family out there who were just so generous. Again I had been rescued from the rain.

It was still a week before Christmas as I headed west for the 200 miles to San Antonio. I knew that I couldn't make it there to my niece's house in only a week, and that I'd be spending Christmas on the road. As a few days went by, it seemed to get colder and mistier. Nights in the tent were warm enough but the days were getting tougher. Not bad enough to seek shelter, just far from the fun of a sunny day.

December 24 started out just barely okay. The night before, I had camped in a little triangular spot just big enough for my tent, behind some bushes out of sight. I had 12 miles to go to the town of Sheridan where I hoped there'd be a convenience store. Somehow no one I asked had been quite sure whether there was one there or not. Supposedly there was a Dairy Queen but it was not likely open on Christmas Eve. I had walked most of the way to Sheridan when the rain started. I put on my windbreaker for protection on my top half, but I wasn't really ready when it came to my feet. You'd think I'd have known better by now, but between the drought in the southeast and dodging the rain at some host's homes, I hadn't really been caught in the rain until now.

There I was, only three miles to go to Sheridan, figuring I could tough it out. I really didn't have a choice. Three miles go by quickly in a warm dry car, but walking, it takes an hour, and I was anything but warm and dry.

As the rain came down, soaking my feet more and more, an SUV passed me, then made a U-turn and came back along the road toward me. The SUV stopped next to me. I opened the passenger door and the woman driving simply said, "Get in!" I wasn't going to debate the issue. Although I hadn't accepted any rides from strangers along the road, I knew I needed rescuing again. I was pretty miserable and after all it was Christmas Eve. In the SUV were Tanya Beyette and her 6-year-old daughter, Abby. They were headed back to their home in Sheridan. Tanya said she would help me find a place for the night, which sounded pretty good to me. We came into the small town and there was an ice cream place, closed of course, but it had a protected overhang and a picnic table. I told Tanya that I'd be okay there, at least I'd be out of the rain. She said she'd try to do better for me.

Out to her house we drove. She apologized that she really didn't have room in her small house. Her husband, she explained, understood how she was always bringing home strays (Xena and I were strays!), but on Christmas Eve, she didn't want to ask him to move over. We considered the stable next to her home and again I said I'd be fine with that. The irony of it being a stable on Christmas Eve didn't escape me.

I just wanted to get into my warm sleeping bag and get some sleep. "Let me check one more place," she said, turning back toward town and driving to her local church. Tanya went into the church for a minute, leaving the heater on in the car. I chatted a little with Abby who was in the back with Xena and my pack. The girl leaned forward and said to me, "You know, I was the one who told my mom she just *had* to pick you up!" I thanked her. I suppose we both knew that her mom probably would have stopped anyway, but I guess the girl wanted me to know she had insisted. I just sat there with my hands in front of the heater vent, so grateful to be warm. Tanya quickly returned from the church, got in and told me she'd found me a place. She drove me to a small house in town where an older man welcomed me in. Ironically, he had seen me earlier that day. He had spoken with me at the convenience store 12 miles back.

The man's name was Dewey Kemp. He had a propane space heater going in the living room. I didn't move away from it for about an hour. We watched a football game and he told me his war stories from Korea, or maybe it was Vietnam. This was one tough dude, but he had opened his home to me. I listened to all he had to say and watched the game too. Xena and I bunked down for the night in that small house and we woke up warm and dry on Christmas morning. Many Christmases have brought me joy and warmth through the years, but I have never been more grateful for the simple grace I found that day.

Blog entry December 25: *Hello. Merry Christmas to all! It's Christmas Day, and I'm about 75 miles east of San Antonio, where I will visit my niece, Becky, her husband and kids for about a week after New Year's, and for my birthday. I'll be 66 on January 3rd. Not bragging, not complaining. It just is.*

I left early Christmas morning. The rain had subsided and I was off to Hallettsville, a much bigger town. There, I had been told, were several convenience stores. I was very happy. I had lucked out.

On the way to Hallettsville, however, I had a reversal, literally. I had stopped along the road and decided to go down under a bridge to eat my lunch. It was usually nicer down under a bridge. There was usually water for Xena to drink and to play in, although she rarely went in above her ankles, and the view for me was much more peaceful than any view up along the road. I finished my lunch and came back up to the road and headed off again. About two miles later I saw a sign that said, "Sublime—4 miles." The problem was that I had seen the same sign, facing the other direction, only four miles back. A brief flash of confusion passed as I quickly realized what had happened. I had just been walking in the wrong direction! Now if someone's driving and you go a couple miles out of your way, it's not that big a deal. Even in the big picture of my entire walk it shouldn't seem like that much. But when you're expecting, on a chilly, damp Christmas Day, that you've been making progress, it's a bit hard to accept such a reversal.

What I had done was that I had come up from the bridge and forgot that I had crossed the road to go down to the creek. I had headed off in the direction that would have been right if I had gone down under on my side of the road. This realization did not exactly leave me in the holiday spirit. I decided immediately that the only thing to relieve the sense of loss would be to try to hitchhike four miles to make up for my blunder. I accepted this as a reasonable way to get back to where I should be, four miles farther down the road. So I turned around and now put out my thumb, a hitchhiker with a dog on Christmas afternoon.

I walked two more miles before anyone stopped. Finally, a man in a pickup pulled over and offered me a ride. I got in and told him about my walk, how I had gone the wrong direction, and that I only wanted a four-mile lift. He offered to take me the nine miles or so to Hallettsville but I told him no thanks, I just wanted to resume my regular walk. He was surprised that I wouldn't take his more generous, longer offer.

This man was Buddy Whitley, and before I got out, he told me two things. First he told me he'd been driving the other direction earlier and had seen me on the road. He was concerned because, with Xena leading me down the road, he thought maybe I was blind. Secondly, he said that when he first saw me, he had been on his way to his Christmas dinner. He had arrived there, and sat down to the dinner table only to excuse himself after a few minutes. He had got up and left his dinner to come back and offer me a ride.

Buddy drove only the four miles I had asked for. I was back on schedule thanks to a man who was moved by his concern for a stranger alone on the road. Maybe because it was Christmas. Maybe, but I had the feeling that on most any day, his heart would have led him in the same direction. What a gift!

I made it to Hallettsville late in the afternoon. At that time of year, that meant it was almost dark. After my typical snack of an ice cream sandwich at the first store, I headed on through town unsure whether I would make it to a camping spot outside the city limits or if I'd have to hole up somewhere in town. The church in the middle of town had an electronic sort of carillon playing Christmas carols. It was all rather festive.

A fairly large bridge crossed a fairly dinky creek, as I recall, and I realized that under that bridge on a Christmas night I'd be out of any more rain and probably no one would know I was there. It was already dark. Xena and I quietly made camp. Cheese and crackers made my meal once I had gotten in my two sleeping sacks (the inner one was like a lining of polyester mesh, which I'd recommend to anyone in cold weather). As I lay there listening to the carols, I was warm and full. Maybe I could have fallen asleep listening to them, but they were plenty loud, echoing down there under the bridge. Then, after some beautiful instrumental carols, the church changed CDs or whatever, switching to an album done by some country singer. This fellow, it seemed, was determined to recreate every known carol, spicing up everything from "Away in a Manger" to "Frosty the Snowman" with his own signature country twang.

Now I'm not a fan of country music, and I was very tired. It had gotten to be about 10:30 at night. The singer, probably some famous guy named Travis Brett or something, launched into "Rudolph the Red-Nosed Reindayer" (not a misspelling). I was fidgeting. The church wasn't far away so I couldn't tune out and just go to sleep. I was Travis' captive audience, as was most of the town.

After several more songs, along came "Silent Night." If you've never heard this classic done with a Texas drawl, well let me tell you... I found myself in deep prayer that Christmas night. I was praying the music would stop. The last line of the carol of course is "Sleep in Heavenly Peace." How I was praying for just that. It's repeated twice at the end of the song. To my astonishment, and within a moment, to my great delight, old Travis got to the second "sleep in heavenly" and the last word never came. There was no "peace" at the end of the carol but there was peace in my tent. The carillon went quiet for the night.

I had to laugh. I had enjoyed the last two days, cold and wet, but then warm and dry. My Christmas was over. For New Year's I hoped to be with family in San Antonio. I closed my eyes and slept soundly.

Looking back, I have realized that it was there in Hallettsville that the balance between "struggle" and "fun" had finally started to even out. I was actually starting to have a lot of fun.

Walking west through Shiner and Gonzales to Seguin was uneventful. It was cold of course, but by now I was accustomed to it. I lost a tooth in this stretch, but otherwise I was okay. My son had arranged another couch-surfing event for me. At this point, I was still a day from my niece's house, but when a woman, Sherrie Reimers, phoned to offer me a place to stay on New Year's Eve, I jumped at the chance. What really surprised me was that she said she was out of state and wouldn't return for a few days but that the door was open and I could just go in and make myself at home. Can you imagine? As a complete stranger, I was being welcomed into someone's empty home! Sherrie would be moving in a couple weeks but most of her furniture was still there, she said, including a bed for me.

That day it was still a long walk to her house, including an extra mile south off my walking route. By the time I headed off the highway toward her place, it was getting dark. I hadn't gone a hundred yards down that side road to her house when an SUV stopped and the woman driving asked if I needed a ride. I said sure, I was only going another mile and this short stretch wasn't on my official path anyway. I got in. Her name was Susan and it turned out she was friends with Sherrie. By the time we reached Sherrie's house, Susan had offered to take me to dinner. I settled in and took a shower. An hour later we were on our way to the IHOP restaurant for an excellent New Year's Eve dinner and an incredible conversation with our waitress. She was a young woman absolutely devoted to her children and talked with us through most of our meal. I didn't write down her name, but when I get through there again, I'll stop in to say hello.

Susan and I had a great time. My New Year's Eve, which I thought would be totally boring, turned out special after all. Before dropping me off, Susan offered to drive me the next morning from Sherrie's across San Antonio to the west side of town where my niece lived. I said goodnight and reveled in the knowledge that I would make it to Becca's on New Year's Day. Again I slept soundly.

So I accepted that ride across San Antonio. That city was one of about five urban areas where, thanks to a couch-surfing host with a car, I was able to avoid the serious problems of crossing a big city with a dog and, after San Antonio, with a cart as well. Big city traffic, city intersections and expressways are dangerous, and an encumbered hiker becomes a traffic hazard. I make no apologies for these short rides. I believe that avoiding those urban scenes was a very good, safe idea. Becca's home is on the west side of San Antonio so the city was now behind me. Half my walk across America was over. Now it was time to rest and recharge!

Others Along the Way
East Texas

-Quanina, who stopped along the road, gave me a small pull-cart to try out and also gave me a donation.
-The nice lady at the Shell in Mauriceville.
-Steve Mayes, a birder at the Sabine Woods birding site.
-Jay Long at the Nome convenience store.
-The three nice young folks by the stuck truck before Devers.
-Nice lady at the Devers convenience store.
-Tasha and friend at the Raymond convenience store—gave me pizza!
-Wanda at the Ames convenience store.
-Clay Wickesser and his kids who talked to me for a while. As I started to leave, Clay came back to give me a special nickel that he had always carried. It has a cross cut out of the middle of it. I still have it.
-Judy LaRue and Lynn Baker in Liberty, gave me a bag of dog food and some sandwiches. Those I don't still have. We ate them.
-Britney, Thomas and Laney, outside the CVS, generous.
-The O'Briens, walking.
-Judy at the Rosenberg Burger King.
-Everett, a young man at Auto Sales in Rosenberg, appreciates the birds.
-Susan and Benny at Sunny's before East Bernard.
-Christina at East Bernard Exxon.
-The young family who offered me a ride in their blue pickup.

-The Supaks and their granddaughter Taylor at the Subway in East Bernard.

-Sharon, who bought my sandwich at that same Subway.

-The owner and staff at "The Cafe" in East Bernard.

-Kymbra at the Dollar General in Eagle Lake.

-Willie Freeland who stopped along the road to give me the hot coffee and cookies. I think they were things he had bought for himself. That made my morning!

-Judy at the post office in Altair, generous.

-B.J. and Brenda at Sonny's in Rock Island.

-Everett Moore, along the road, generous.

-Pastor Nick Williams who stopped to talk.

-Young man in the blue pickup with two girls, who asked, "What do you need?"

-Gary and Mercedes the cashier at the Shell in Hallettsville.

-Mor and Vadi, along the road in Shiner.

-Shanta at the Tiger Tote in Shiner.

-Michelle Ansel at the Dollar General in Shiner.

-Jolyn at the Tiger Tote in Gonzalez.

-The two dudes who stopped to get a picture of Xena.

-John and Mary Pool and Katrina Messenger in Gonzalez.

-Larry Davis, Rachel and the kids, unusually nice people.

-Kenneth Riedel, surveying, good conversation.

-Bob Wallish, generous.

-Viola, Angel and Aubrey, generous.

-Corey, who offered a ride.

-Tony and Cindy, generous, and gave dog treats for Xena.

-Irene, generous.

-Ryan and Vivian Darnell and the kids, generous.

-Leslie and Macey, generous.

-Bart, generous, and gave me dog food.

CHAPTER 11

Becca's House ✒ My Halftime Break
January 1-16

And so, after 1,200 miles, I arrived at Becca's home. She and her husband Nathan have four kids: Mark, Michaela, Kayte and Kade. Mark gave up his room to me for two weeks and never complained even subtly, which for a teenager, I thought was remarkable. I moved in, rested and regrouped, and even celebrated my 66th birthday there.

As soon as the birthday cake was gone, I made a quick decision; while I was on a break at Becca's, I had the opportunity to retrieve my van from Alabama. I realized that if I could get it to Becca's, it would be that much closer to the end of my walk. Almost on the spur of the moment, I decided to grab a small pack, leave Xena running happily in Becca's big fenced backyard, and take a bus all the way back to Montgomery. After 24 hours of an uneventful but typical bus ride, I found myself at the south side of the capital of Alabama. I was still a good 35 miles from my van at Rob's house, northwest of Montgomery. I had hoped there'd be city busses running up through town, but no such luck. I had to hitchhike. And walk.

Now, I've had some experience with both of those methods of travel, but I was tired from the bus trip. I have to admit that at 7 AM, I was discouraged and unsure how tough it was going to be. I walked a ways and asked a guy at a gas station to give me a ride. For five dollars he took me about five miles. Then I got lucky. The car that stopped next was decked out in Pittsburgh Steelers colors and souvenirs. I've been a fan of that football team for a long time, so I had to laugh that here in the middle of Alabama, I was being rescued by a Steeler's fan. He even introduced himself to me by the name he said everyone called him: "Pittsburgh!" We talked football and I rode with him into Prattville, which was as far as he was going. That was great, but I still had 18 miles to go. I decided at that point that the expense of a cab would be well worth it. I was in no mood to quibble with myself. I wanted to get where I was going, this time as fast as I could. The cab came and got me, so late that afternoon I walked in the dirt road to Rob's, and there in the garage, I saw my van. I made sure it would start. It did. I went to bed.

I spent one day in town, then started the two-day drive back to San Antonio. It felt weird to drive some of the same roads I had walked, but mostly it was just interstate driving and *presto!* I was back at Becca's.

That side trip still seems unreal to me, it went by so fast. In writing this, I almost forgot I had done it, but it made a big difference at the end of my walk. For the rest of my trip, I would now know that all I had to do was to get back to Becca's and I'd be driving my own wheels again.

It was great fun to be part of Becca's rambunctious family, playing with the kids and watching some TV. But most importantly, while I was there, I got together a cart to take with me on the rest of the walk. I knew I wouldn't be able to backpack all the food and especially all the water that I was going to need between those widely-separated western towns and through long desert areas.

I had spoken on the phone to that young man named Anthony who, I found out, would complete his similar walk within a few weeks. He had used a cart starting back in

Mississippi. He described his cart and some modifications he had made to it. I bought the exact same cart and with Nathan's help, assembled it and reinforced the handles, which Anthony had recommended.

Blog entry January 6, 2012: *I have bought a Schwinn bike trailer which converts to a covered stroller. I'll push this contraption as I walk west. It's the only way to carry enough food and water for several days for me and my hound. I don't really like the way it makes me look more like a homeless guy, with a grocery cart or something. I may wear my backpack anyway just so I won't look like such a weenie. Maybe I'll fill the backpack with helium balloons. No one would know and I'd still appear like the macho adventurer I want to be. But still I think the cart looks silly, oh well. Like I said, dire circumstances.*

The cart is designed to be a bike trailer that carries toddlers. It converts to a stroller big enough for a little one to sit with plenty of room. It has two 20" bike wheels on the sides and a small wheel in front on an extended arm. Nathan suggested we remove the arm and mount the small wheel directly on the front bar of the cart. That was absolutely brilliant. It made a huge difference not having that 18" nose sticking out, ready to catch on most anything. Anthony also had suggested getting solid rubber inserts for the bike wheels, thereby guaranteeing no flats. My son Isaac checked the Internet and found them in stock at a local outlet. Anthony said that it was hard to get the inserts into the tires, that it had taken him and a friend an hour to install each of the two inserts. Nathan, working with great determination, got each one in in about 20 minutes. It wasn't the first time I've watched a young man do something that I probably couldn't do. I realized how lucky I was to have his help. I started practice-loading my cart and pushing it up and down the rural road in front of their home.

While in San Antonio, I visited the Mitchell Lake Audubon Center. There I met Susan Albert and Iliana Pena, who gave me a birding tour of the preserve and an overview of all that their office does to coordinate state-wide Audubon activities, especially those efforts relating to the drought conditions and water usage that I had learned about in Houston. Iliana has been particularly involved in the legal efforts and the monitoring of the whooping crane population at Aransas. Without devoted staff in these environmentally-conscious organizations, our natural world would suffer greatly.

Since Theodore Roosevelt originally set aside public lands to be protected as federal refuges, forests and parks, there has been a continuing effort to safeguard the beauty and diversity of life in our wilderness areas, which are often in our own back yards. The Audubon Society has been at the forefront of these efforts.

(Update: On March 10, 2013, U.S. District Court Judge Janis Graham Jack found that the Texas Commission for Environmental Quality had violated the Endangered Species Act by failing to provide adequate freshwater inflow to the whooping crane habitat. This legal victory for the birds is expected to stand!)

The first two weeks of January were pretty cold and raw. Several of those days I would have been miserable walking so I was quite happy to hang out with Becca's great family, eating well and relaxing. I knew, however, that I had to get moving. Not only was it going to be getting a lot warmer before I would get to California, but the longer a person is away from doing something hard, the scarier it becomes. I had to jump back in and start swimming again.

Early on January 17, Becca dropped me off at the main road out of her town. I took a picture of the beautiful clouds right there at that intersection. Those clouds seemed to be welcoming me to the western half of my trip. I truly felt that they were saying that everything was going to be all right. So, off I went toward Uvalde and Del Rio, taking the southern road, Route 90, near the border and well south of the interstate. I knew that before long, I'd be looking at the mountains of Mexico, far away, but really just across the Rio Grande.

CHAPTER 12

Our Trip 🐕 Xena's View
Translated by Brad from her dictation

Brad: Since it's "halftime," I thought this would be a good place to include Xena's version of the trip. I swear it's unedited. She has a right to express her opinions.

The first of the following blog entries was written during the oppressive heat in Georgia, when Xena was uncomfortable in all that fur; the second is from much later, in Texas.

Blog entry September 30: *Xena report; she's not doing too bad for a draftee. She never volunteered for this. She drives me crazy, lurching after lizards or moles as we walk. Whenever we see horses, cows or other dogs, she strains at the leash to visit and play, which of course I can't allow. Her body language is pretty clear. Sometimes she'll hang back when she's tired, just enough to pull on the leash a little and let me know she's doing all of this against her free will.*

Blog entry January 30: *I've taken to singing to Xena, my version of the theme from "Cops." It goes "Bad dog, bad dog. What you gonna do when they come for you? Bad dog, bad dog..."*

Xena: I think I had a good time. It's been six months now since we finished and you may know, if you have a dog, that we canines don't really think much about the past, or for that matter, the future. When pressed, I can remember quite a bit, but it's a struggle. It's not that we can't remember, it's just that the past is gone. There's so much happening now. And the future? Forget the future! Past and future just seem irrelevant, but Brad is writing this book and thought I could add my thoughts and recollections, limited as they might be.

While we were taking short hikes before the walk, I remember him saying something about going for a really long walk. He drew out the word "long" for emphasis. I figured that would be great. I love walks. When we were in upstate New York last year, we'd walk through the woods and I wasn't even on the leash or as I prefer to call it the "lead." I prefer to call it that because I do most of the leading. Off the lead, I loved being able to run free and explore the forest and I made sure I never got out of earshot of Brad. After all, he's my human and he gets worried if he can't at least hear me. If he calls and I don't hear right away, he starts thinking I've gotten lost or whatever, maybe that something happened to me. But my sense of smell is of course incredible and I never get out of nose-range!

I've always been able to handle myself around other animals. In New York there didn't seem to be any dangers in the woods. Anyway, I was running free up there. I guess that's where I picked up Lyme disease from some tick, but I was never sick from it, I just had to take medicine.

For me, the one thing that was really different once we started the walk across the country, was that I was never off the lead. Once or twice we'd be at someone's house and I could run around in a fenced yard, but otherwise night and day I was on a lead. At night, Brad would switch me from the 16-foot retractable lead to the 15-foot steel cable with the red plastic coating on it and the clips at either end. He'd hook me to a tree or a fence post or even just a little bush for the night. He'd put up the tent and go to sleep. I didn't mind. I knew the routine. I had been used to being on a lead like that back in Arkansas where I grew up. There I had to be on a lead because the fence around the yard was not real high and I had jumped over several times. After Brad found me wandering down the middle of the main street in town...well, you get the idea. I had learned to accept my human-imposed limit.

Every morning when we'd start out, Brad would say to me, "All right girl, let's rock'n'roll!" I knew then that we were in for another day, bound together for another adventure. I know now that being tethered together on our walk for those seven months was important, so I put up with it. I'm not real smart around cars I guess. I can take 'em or leave 'em, so to speak. I don't chase them but I'm also not afraid of them like maybe I should be. I suppose I could have gotten run over chasing a squirrel or suddenly crossing the road to see another dog or something. So I guess Brad was keeping me safe in the day and at night too. There were times at night when the howl of coyotes might have lured me away from the tent and I don't know what that might have led to. And out west there was something called mountain lions which we never saw, but Brad seemed pretty anxious alone in those desert areas when there were mountain slopes close by.

I really am pretty attached to Brad. He's been the only constant in my life. He feeds me and cares for me and hugs me a lot. I think the thing I like most is that he doesn't try to control me too much. He says I'm a "wild woman" and he likes me that way. I couldn't get too wild all tethered up all the time, but he'd let me sniff and he'd let me look at horses (my favorite) and cows (my second favorite) and goats, cats, pigs, whatever. I didn't have to "heel" across America, I kind of roamed at the end of the 16-foot lead mostly.

And another thing. Some people had suggested he harness me to a sled on wheels or some cart or something. I guess me being a husky, everybody thought, "Sure, she's bred for pulling." Well, I'm glad he didn't do that. This walk wasn't my idea! Besides, I think it would have been weird along most roadsides pulling a wagon or something. I would have had to have been on a lead anyway and I bet we could have logistical problems in the way of entanglements or traffic issues. (Bet you thought I didn't know words like logistical, didn't you?) I did carry a pack, however. I didn't like it at first but I got used to it. It made me feel that I was pulling my own weight, like I was part of the team.

So we started out at that nice quiet beach in Georgia and even though lots of different things happened in the next seven months, every day was really just the same. At least mostly and at least for me. You see, I'm a dog. I don't spend any time thinking, "Boy, yesterday was rough," or "Hey, how much farther is it to the next convenience store?" Those things don't really matter. You just walk. And sniff. You sniff the air, you sniff the ground, you watch out for traffic, you get really tired, you rest, you get back up and walk some more. It really doesn't matter how far the next store is and it certainly isn't worth worrying about. I tried to tell Brad that, and sometimes I think he got the idea. He said that he appreciated that about me. But he is human.

Humans plan; when they plan, they worry whether they have planned enough. They also worry about whether they did okay yesterday. To me, all that is basically useless.

I just like to walk. I like to feel my feet hitting the ground, my muscles rippling along, and I like to breathe the multi-scented air, the atmosphere we live in. I liked hearing the train whistles and the barking of friendly dogs. I did not like the sound of the semis coming by, often too close to us. I got burs in my feet, mostly out in the desert. They really hurt and I couldn't always chew them out. Brad would stop and make me give him my paw and he'd pull them out. Other than that, I had no trouble with my feet.

I met a lot of people and many gave me treats, even meat sometimes. I mean a couple of times people even bought me a hamburger. Being a vegetarian, Brad would forget how much I like meat. As we'd be walking along the side of the road, I'd spot something dead and scarf it right up. I'd be trying to wolf it down when Brad would stop and pull me over, grab my jaws and make me spit it out. I hated that but I never bit him or even growled but I certainly resisted. Sometimes I would get it swallowed before he could get it, but usually he would get it out and say something like, "Ew, girl, what the heck—leave that alone!" He'd pull that morsel out of my mouth and then throw it out of my reach. Dang! He claimed he didn't know how it had died, whatever it was.

Well I can tell you how it died—10 miles from the nearest town, out along a highway—well, duh! It got runned over! It wasn't poisoned! I missed some tasty treats that way. Sometimes, especially with bones and bony stuff, he'd say, "Okay, girl, you can have it!" Then I'd keep walking, happily munching my unidentifiable but delicious prize.

The rain didn't bother me. I'm a Siberian husky after all. I love snow and even sleet. I can sleep in the stuff. My feet don't even get cold. Nothing really bothered me that much. Early on, Brad tried to put some salve on my feet. His sister-in-law had given it to him; apparently she used it on her dogs. I didn't want it. I'd lick off the little bit he put on and wrestle away from him. He would finally give up and say, "All right, if your feet get sore, don't come crying to me!" Me? Crying about sore feet? The crying about foot pain wasn't coming from me, get it?

Some people even asked Brad if he had considered doggy shoes for me. Doggy shoes? O Lord, I would have been so embarrassed if any other dogs had seen me wearing "booties!" At least that never even got tried!

I mentioned that I liked the people we met. So many people noticed me way before they noticed Brad. I guess that's because I'm such a cool-looking dog. I know that sounds kinda uppity but huskies are a real classic-looking dog. I have those whitish, almost steely-blue/whitish eyes that everybody loves. If I heard, "Oh, what a beautiful dog!" once, I heard it probably five times a day. I didn't mind. Most people wanted to pet me and stroke my fur and look at my eyes. Some kids (and adults too!) were afraid of me because I look like a wolf. Maybe they fear all dogs, I don't know, but most people would fawn all over me and want to take my picture. "Oh my! Look at those eyes!" they'd say, camera in hand. They'd want me to look straight at them. "Xena! Xena! Xena!" I usually wouldn't look at them. I think my profile is actually better, so I'd just turn a little to the side.

But I think it was good I was with Brad—not just to attract positive attention to him and to this momentous walk we were on, but because, I think, I was probably more of a protection to him than either of us realized. We'll never know if anybody left him alone because they saw a "wolf" with him. Maybe several, maybe none. Like I said, we'll never know. I do remember chasing off a skunk one night. He only sprayed me a little and Brad said I'd probably kept that skunk from tearing his way into Brad's tent.

In the end, everything turned out right and it made me feel good. I know I did my part and I didn't have to pull no "sled" to be valuable. Also, Brad talked to me. A lot. I know he needed that. So did I, for that matter. He's my buddy.

I think Brad's writing about most of the things we saw and did on the trip. That's good, because for me it was just an endless movie of sunrise, sunset and night, horses and cars, gravel and grass.

Sometimes I'd be tied to a cactus at night or once in a while would sleep in the small bathroom of some cheap motel. I remember seeing rivers and mountains and oceans and trees and trains and clouds and stores and trucks, but I really couldn't tell you where they were. I'll leave that up to Brad. He's pretty good at that human stuff. I know I had a good time. He and I hardly ever argued. Sometimes I'd yank hard suddenly on the lead when I'd see a mouse running along in the grass. Once I almost toppled Brad into a ditch filled with water. He hollered at me pretty good that time, but it didn't last long. I'd try to remember to not do that but do you know how hard it is to resist natural impulses? We made it all the way, and I hadn't caused any harm. Brad says he couldn't have done the walk without me; I know he means it.

We had a great time. When we got to the Pacific Ocean, Brad must have arranged somehow for about a hundred dogs to meet us at the beach there in San Diego. Some place called

"Dog Beach." That I do remember! We were done and I was surrounded by lots of friends. I started out saying, "I think I had a good time." I guess that, really, I had a *great* time. I loved it, and I might consider doing it again, but then, who thinks about the future?

In West Texas. The only place to hide for the night.

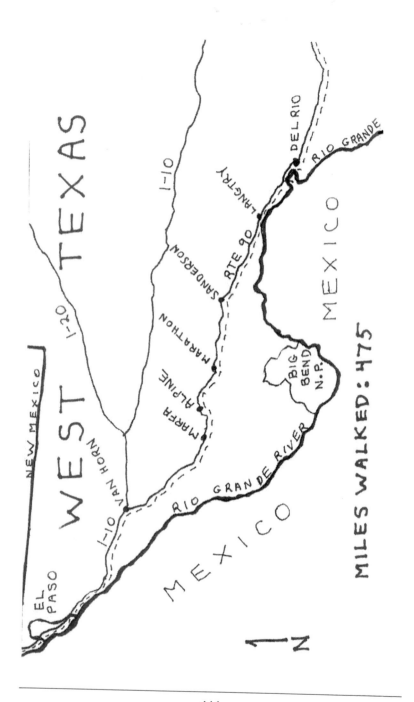

TEXAS

WEST

NEW MEXICO

EL PASO

I-20

I-10

VAN HORN

MARFA

ALPINE

MARATHON

SANDERSON

RTE 90

LANGTRY

DEL RIO

RIO GRANDE

I-10

I-10

BIG BEND N.P.

RIO GRANDE RIVER

MEXICO

MEXICO

MILES WALKED: 475

N

114

CHAPTER 13

Starting the Second Half
January 17

Blog entry January 17: *I was pretty tired when reaching San Antonio, and now I'm ready to go again on to the most difficult part of my trip. Nathan helped me so much, converting and strengthening my cart. He has good understanding of tools and mechanics and now I'm in good shape, cart wise. Becca cooked special veggie meals for me and sent me packing with cookies and brownies and cough syrup for this cedar allergy everybody down here has. All four kids were fun to be with, at Kaela's basketball games, riding bikes with Kayte, getting my dog pack fixed by Mark or just playing with Kade. I miss the tub, the T.V., the bed and the food. But mostly, I miss their family.*

Leaving San Antonio was momentous. I now had a cart to deal with out on the open road. The western roads are actually better in that they have generally wider berms for walking, but many times I'd find myself pushing the cart through low grass or gravel for stretches at a time whenever the traffic crowded me. I hadn't gone far, maybe 50 miles, when the front wheel of the cart (which was actually two small wheels set together at angles downward in a "V" shape) began to wear out. Those two plastic wheels were breaking around their thin axle and were refusing to track straight. I knew that this was something that wasn't going to work all the way to California.

Outside a small store near Uvalde, I saw a Goodwill-type donation bin. Next to the bin, donated, was another cart/stroller remarkably similar to mine. It had a front wheel on a long bar, but this was a very sturdy single wheel. I knew this was very much like a miracle. I had to get this cart, get the wheel off it and at least carry it along with me. Inside the store, the clerk gave me the number of the charity group who owned the donation box. I called them and got the OK to take the cart. I promised them a donation. Next door was an auto shop. I had them remove the wheel, which required power tools. I took the wheel and gave them the cart. I had no idea how I'd mount the wheel because the connections weren't exactly the same, but I couldn't go much farther with the original wheels. I don't think the guys at the auto shop were into mounting it for me; they were pretty busy. I headed on to the town of Brackettville where I hoped to find a hardware store and spend the time and energy doing the job myself.

I made it to Brackettville on a rainy afternoon. I stopped in at the sheriff's office to ask where I might camp for the night. The sheriff let me put up my tent under the shed that protects his squad cars. I felt safe and I was dry. The next morning I bought some metal and plastic parts at the hardware store. I asked the clerk if I might pay someone to drill a couple of holes for me. The clerk said that the owner probably could do that.

The owner was David Mann. He came with his tools to the police shed, we got the holes drilled and the wheel attached, all for no charge. He was glad to help. Not only did he do all that, he also offered me a place to sleep inside that night on the floor of his workout gym. I was so grateful. I was now ready for lots more miles.

As I headed west from Brackettville the next day, I could tell that the new wheel was going to work well. It would eventually need some more work down the road, but for now, it worked. Mr. Mann made it happen. Again I was renewed.

I had first begun having some anxiety about being so close to the Mexican border as far back as East Texas. There's a lot of Mexican migrants moving east along the highways and even through open country, with everyone trying to get as far as possible from the Rio Grande. Now approaching Del Rio, a good-sized town directly on the border, my anxieties picked up a bit more. I had asked the border patrol if there was anything I needed to know. They told me I was in more danger from traffic than from people. The border patrol has a very strong presence along the border, stretching all the way to California.

I had driven through this area many times on my birding travels and had been in Del Rio and in West Texas many times, but I always had my van for protection. Being in my tent each night was a very different story. I knew that the Mexicans coming for work weren't going to bother me; they didn't want to have any contact with anyone, unless maybe they needed water. But the idea of gun-runners and drug smugglers, that worried me a bit. Mostly those guys didn't want any contact either. Sometimes they'd steal or hijack a car or truck or maybe break into a home, but that didn't happen often. I doubted they'd have any interest in my tent or my dog. I just tried to relax.

One late afternoon on a long empty stretch of highway with little vegetation, I decided to camp under a large concrete bridge. The bridge provided shelter from the wind, from precipitation and from the view of any passing traffic. I tied Xena to one of the big concrete pillars holding up the bridge and set up my tent a few feet from her. As usual near dark, I climbed into my tent and began to rack out for the night.

Before I fell asleep, I began to hear voices from far off. Out there, well away from the nearest town, hearing human voices was unusual, to say the least. I was dreading the sound of those voices and my entire attention went to trying to figure out what was happening. The conversation got louder and closer and finally, as I recognized only Spanish being spoken, this small group of men came directly under the bridge. They came directly toward my tent, and though I couldn't see from in my tent, I realized they had sat down on some exposed concrete only about 15 feet from me.

Xena had given a warning bark. She seemed alert but okay. I was glad she had barked. My visitors knew that I had a dog, but they also knew that she was tied and that I was in my tent. I called out from in my sleeping bag in my best American Spanish, "Hola!" They answered back, and then in what sounded like high spirits, went on talking together. I decided I should maybe ask a little more.

I interrupted their conversation asking, "Tu quieras dormire aqui?" which I hoped meant, "Do you want to sleep here?" and not "Do you want me to sleep with your daughter on her waterbed?" or something equally provocative. I guess I was close enough to the right words. They didn't laugh but simply answered, "Oh, Si, Si!" Somehow I understood their next question which asked if that would be okay with me. As if I was going to say, "Well, no. This is my bridge! You'll have to leave!" Of course instead I said something like, "Es ist okay con mi." Again they didn't laugh. I hoped they were satisfied with our little conversation. I just lay there, listening intently, all thoughts of falling asleep being put off indefinitely.

For the next one or two hours, these gentlemen (I couldn't tell if there were three or four of them) hung out, just sitting there on that concrete, laughing, talking and singing. I had to consider the possibility that they were talking about me. Maybe they were having a good old time thinking about what to do to me in the middle of the night or in the morning, but actually I doubted that.

After a while, I began to appreciate their genuinely good vibes. I did not, however, relax enough to fall asleep. One of the men had a cell phone and had been talking on it a lot. None of them seemed like they were bunking down for the night. I couldn't figure out what they were doing. I guess I'm pretty naive or else I was just too worried to think it through. These guys were just waiting for a ride. The cell phone guy had made contact and they all were just waiting under an obvious landmark, out of sight from the road.

After about two hours, I heard a vehicle come to a sliding stop up on the bridge. My new friends, without even an "Adios, Amigo!" all ran up onto the bridge. Car doors opened and closed and all I heard was that vehicle quickly taking off heading back east. As the sound of that truck faded in the distance, my breathing returned to normal. I smiled at the thought of my vulnerability and how magnified it had seemed in that situation. I called out, "Good girl!" to Xena and began to relax. Soon I was sound asleep.

In two more days, I was walking the urban streets of Del Rio, a town I had often visited while birding. Del Rio has one of the most beautiful river walks anywhere; as I passed through on a warm afternoon, I saw dozens of kids playing and swimming in the clear water that springs up at the north end of that river walk. It felt great to see that town again. Also, I was looking forward to seeing Beth, a friend of mine from Arkansas who was coming down to visit me on my walk. She arrived at midnight at the Del Rio Wal-Mart at the west end of town. I had to unscrew the handles from my cart in order to fit them into her hatchback, which took about a half an hour. I didn't remember, maybe just because I was tired, that the cart could be emptied and then it would fold up. Oh well, we make mistakes.

We camped a few miles away at the Amistad Dam camping area, by the enormous lake created by the dam. The next day, we drove out to the Pecos River crossing west of town. This river crossing is a very high bridge over a wide river canyon. Out on the bridge, you can see for miles in each direction. You can watch the slow flow of the Pecos heading south to the Rio Grande at the Mexican border only a few miles away. There is usually a large flock of black vultures sitting in the morning sun or circling overhead in the afternoons. And often you can hear the loud descending trill of the canyon wren; the sound is beautiful and unmistakable, echoing off the canyon walls, all coming from a four-inch bird! I accepted the ride from Beth to this spot so that she could see this amazing dramatic crossing. On the far side of the bridge, I reassembled my cart, said good-bye, and took off again, heading now into some seriously open territory.

The next town was Langtry. It boasts the original "courtroom" of "Judge" Roy Bean, "the Law West of the Pecos." The town was named for George Langtry, a civil engineer who worked for the railroad, but legend has it that Bean named the town after British stage actress and celebrity

Lily Langtry. All this was a hundred years ago. The town has changed only a little, now housing a visitor's center. The desert surrounding the town hasn't changed at all. I took some tourist-type pictures of the courtroom and the visitor's center, but there was no store, no ice cream sandwiches in "downtown" Langtry. For that, it's another barren mile to the very west edge of town. There you find a store that seems in the middle of nowhere. The friendly owner charges passers-by some pretty good prices for drinks, snacks, or even a hot sandwich. He needs make no apology out there for high prices. He's the only game in town. I didn't mind his prices at all and besides I got fresh water from him out of the hose. I took off and walked on two more days through Pumpville and Dryden, and another day toward Sanderson.

The railroads wove in and out along the highway. Sometimes they'd be within 20 or 30 yards, sometimes miles away, but they rarely disappeared from sight and even then, I could always hear them powering their way through the desert. For Xena and me, they were our only company.

Others Along the Way
Starting West Texas

-Nancy Barrett and Luann Caywood, generous.
-Phillip and Pete at Hondo Ag Supply.
-Lisa and John, who watched Xena while I went in Wal-Mart; they gave her dog treats and also donated!
-Candy and Melinda, on the road.
-Bob Stewart in D'Hanis.

-Tinka in D'Hanis, offered a place to stay.

-Pearl, a customer at the Knippa store who bought me lunch.

-Naomi, also a customer there who gave me canned pineapple.

-Albert Talamantez, a truck driver at Wal-Mart in Uvalde.

-Delia and Reuben in Uvalde, generous.

-Rock'n'Roll man and his wife in Uvalde, generous.

-Scott Clark, Audubon member, generous.

-Some man in the line behind me in a convenience store who, while I ran from the counter back out to my cart when I realized I had left my wallet sitting out on top of the cart, paid for a new Texas road atlas I left sitting on the counter. The counter guy told me, "The guy behind you paid for the atlas and your ice cream sandwich." I never saw the guy.

-Bryan Hale, Audubon member, generous.

-Letitia, Ben Vasquez and the whole Sheriff's department in Brackettville.

-Lucille Fuentes in Brackettville, paid for my laundry and gave me a book.

-Renee at the Quik-Stop.

-Robert, with FedEx near Laughlin, generous.

-Rosa, nice security guard at the Del Rio Wal-Mart.

-Hoot, another Union Pacific engineer, stopped along the road.

-Richard and Cynthia from South Carolina at the rest stop.

-Dominic and his family from Quebec, at the rest stop.

-And then there was Jeri Barrington, a rancher lady who asked me to say hello to the Pacific Ocean for her, because she doubts she'll ever get to see it. (I made sure I did.) I hope she gets to see it herself someday.

-Cheryl Autry and Billy Johnson, in a pickup before Sanderson.

-And then there was Tara Witt at a rest area who charged my phone from her truck! My phone was dead and I had no way to contact my couch-surf host. While it charged we had a great, inspiring conversation. A very special young woman.

-Jeff Alexander, met at the motel. He once walked 1,000 miles pulling a wagon!

-Robert at the west end of Sanderson, who reminded me that from here to El Paso was "all uphill." Thanks, Robert, I needed that.

-Darryl, an Auburn student, on his motorcycle heading for Big Bend National Park.

-Sheriff Joseph Wallace, a good conversation and a free pen!

-Ed and Katie, British bicyclists crossing America.

-Devin and David, each a solo cross-country bicyclist.

-Raqui Hinkley and Jim Street at the Terrell County News Leader in Sanderson. Raqui wrote a nice article about my walk.

CHAPTER 14

Let the Games Begin!

Blog entry February 2: *This is Major Tom to Ground Control. I'm feeling quite impressed. I feel very far out, out here, believe me. I'm playing games on the road regarding how many steps it is between cars going by. The record is 1,400 steps so far. That's more than half a mile! So you can get some idea of how open this territory is. I hope I get to see a civilization again sometime soon. There's not even any coyotes around. I wonder if that's from the drought, anyone know? Is anybody out there? Major Tom, over and out.*

Perhaps the greatest continuous obstacle on my walk turned out to be boredom. I hadn't expected that. The daily routine, the traffic, that endless white line along the side of the road all contributed to an atmosphere that could easily lead to being bored. I'd give a small wave to almost every driver coming toward me, and that helped, but after all, this was a journey of 6 million steps. In numerals that looks like this: 6,000,000! They say that a journey of a thousand miles begins with the first step. That's certainly true, but it's also true that a journey of over 2,400 miles doesn't end until the 6-millionth step! There are a lot of steps in between.

I know there are worse things than being bored. For instance, if anything starts going wrong—making a wrong turn or running low on water or coyotes howling nearby—you might quickly forget about how you'd been wishing that something exciting would happen just to counteract the boredom. You realize you'd happily retreat to the "ho-hum" state, if you could just get past whatever problem has developed. But when you're bored, your mind can start to wander.

In years past, I had sometimes found myself bored while driving. Sometimes I'd play the alphabet game, looking for printed words that started with the letters of the alphabet in succession. When travelling with Lucy, we'd had fun with silly games like "I'm going to California and I'm taking...an alligator, a baboon, and a coyote, etc."

There were few road signs out west in the desert; it was hard to maintain any alphabet game! I found that I had to focus on something else—anything else! What I did on the road was to make up walking games. These games mostly involved counting the number of steps I would take between cars passing me on the road. I'd keep track in my head of these numbers and create little competitions for myself. These games weren't all that satisfying—in fact, they themselves could get downright boring—but it was the best I could come up with. Now the steps you're taking along a highway may not be the most interesting thing in the world, but there were 6 million of them to play around with. Many long days were lightened at least a little by the "excitement" generated by my one-foot-after-another counting games. Without these diversions, an active mind can descend into a stupor, a zombie-like state. This is not actually the best mentality for walking along a highway.

As far as other games went, I didn't even bring a deck of cards. Music would have been entertaining, but on the road there's only one thing you want to be listening to and that's the sounds of what's going on around you. Word puzzles in the daily paper were a welcome relief. Anywhere I sat down along the road or at night in my tent, I could use them to think about something other than how sore my shoulders or my feet were or how far it was to my next convenience store.

If the Olympics ever includes counting-your-steps games, however, I'm ready to compete for the gold.

CHAPTER 15

West Texas and the Railroads
Early February

It hadn't been long after I'd started walking that I developed a love relationship with the railroads. Even back as far as Georgia, the Kansas City Southern railroad was rocketing along, doing the same thing I was. The railroad was following the best path it could find through the countryside, heading west. Its purposes were much loftier than mine. Its job was to deliver tons and tons of freight and occasionally people, to some point far away. For me, well I was just walking, not bearing any of the importance of these great locomotives, four or five of which were often coupled together, pulling 75 to 140 cars. In contrast, I wasn't delivering anything but myself. I had no commercial purpose. I was just observing.

One thing I observed was that between me and the railroad tracks there were almost always trees and bushes. How nice it was to see all of this greenery in the "no-man's" strip of land between the road and the tracks. This strip was usually 20 to 40 feet wide and although technically owned by the railroad, it seemed that no one cared if you were in that area as long as you weren't causing a problem. I'm sure some loyal railroad man might say it's trespassing, but I was never there until dark, and I was hidden from sight of all traffic on the road. No one was likely to know I was there.

I never made fires. I did no cooking. Not once on the entire trip! I simply put up my tent and slept. I had my self-imposed agreement to not cross any fences or go past any "no trespassing" signs. I did really well sticking to that promise. I could only have done it as well as I did because of the railroads.

Night after night, often for over a hundred miles at a time, thanks to the rails, there'd be a nice little grove of trees to slip into as dusk became dark. I could set up my tent, tie Xena up close to the tent, inflate my one small mattress, store my pack inside the tent and climb inside for the night all in the space of about 15 minutes. I would then have a snack and if it was still light enough, maybe do a crossword puzzle from the morning's paper.

Soon the sound of a locomotive would begin to rise from far off. Within a minute or two, the massive engines would be upon my campsite. I would often have to reassure myself, as they bore down on me, that I had not camped directly on the tracks. Seriously. The trains sometimes rumbled along no more than 15 feet from my tent. Travelling between 20 and 60 miles an hour, these behemoths shake the very ground beneath you. You lie there, a quasi-legal visitor in what you hope is a perfect place for the night. Each train passing by rouses you and reminds you of its overwhelming, massive presence.

So the railroads became my friend. I'd wave to the engineers in the day and be comforted/terrorized by the passing trains at night. All across Georgia, Alabama, Mississippi and Louisiana, about 900 miles, the railroads had created a possibility for answering the hardest challenge of my walk—finding a place to sleep.

Somewhere in Texas it seemed that Kansas City Southern was replaced by Union Pacific. Now the landscape was becoming more barren and the no-man's land between me and those steel rails was not so lush. Bushes and trees got smaller and by West Texas had become almost non-existent. It was a little nerve-racking how dependent I was on having cover at night.

Back before San Antonio, where there were still some tree patches along the road, I camped for the night about 25 feet below a high embankment on which the trains ran. As I set up camp, I noticed something orange up near the tracks, so of course I went to check it out. It was a Union Pacific railroad cap, orange with a black bill and a cool little Union Pacific emblem in front. This would be my hat for the rest of the trip. Being orange it was like a protective flag, but just as important, it belonged to my buddy, the good old Union Pacific.

I often counted cars on the trains, sometimes stopping and watching as they went by, sometimes continuing to walk while I counted. If there weren't at least a hundred I felt cheated somehow. Regardless of the length, every train connected with me, grounded me. I felt their power and determination, rocketing through open country and small towns alike. Their mission seemed too important for them to interrupt their progress for anything. They'd simply blow their whistle and barriers would come down, bells would ring, and all other traffic would stop for them. The trains became my model; I too would be hard to stop. I'd watch them rumble on until they were out of sight. I liked the ones going west best; they were leading the way, quickly getting to where it would take me days or weeks to get to.

That orange Union Pacific hat I found turned out to be good fortune. In West Texas, the road would be cut through any hill or small mountain so that the rock faces would tower above me on both sides. I was walking through one of those very road cuts when a man in a small truck stopped across the highway. Smiling, he asked me what I was doing. (I got that question a lot.) I told him I was walking across the United States. He turned off the engine and came over to talk. His name was Jim Davis. There were many people who stopped along the road to talk, but Jim was different. Right away he saw my hat and told me that he was an engineer for Union Pacific. I told him that I'd found the hat alongside the tracks and that it was a prized possession. He told me that the hat was a first-year railroad man's hat, and that they make the new employees wear one for a full year.

Jim invited me to visit him and his wife in the town of Sanderson, still some 20 miles or so away. The following day I made it to Sanderson and gave them a call. Jim wasn't there, he was out driving train, but he and his wife Sandra had decided to put me up in a motel in town and his wife was to take me to dinner. I don't know if that orange hat had anything to do with all this good karma, but it sure didn't hurt! Sandra and I had a nice meal and I got a good night's rest.

West Texas can be quite cold at this time of year. It was February, after all. I was okay, night or day, but I was cold. At night, I alternated between pulling the sleeping bag up over my face completely, and then having only my nose sticking out. My nose would get so cold that I would then pull it back in and suffocate some more. I fantasized about buying a plastic snorkel, like for skin-diving, so that maybe I could breathe nice cool air and yet still keep my nose warm!

In the morning, I wouldn't get out of the tent if, when I stuck my hand out through the zippered door, it was so cold that I knew I'd be miserable just striking my camp. But even after I would finally be brave enough to get out, as I'd be packing up, it would be so cold that my fingers would be balled up inside my gloves, a cheap, fairly thin cotton pair. I know that this wasn't Minnesota in the winter, but even though we were all the way down south in Texas, I was cold. Not frostbitten, just daggone cold. As I walked, I'd watch the sky. In warm weather, I hoped for clouds, counting on their shadows to provide relief. Now in the colder weather, the clouds had become the "enemy" and their passing meant the welcome reappearance of the warming sun. I had never paid so much attention to the ever-changing world above me.

So that next morning, I walked on out of Sanderson, starting the 54 miles of completely barren road to Marathon. The first day I walked about 15 miles, camped in some sparse bushes and woke up the next morning to another cold day. I packed up and had only walked a mile or so when I heard a car from behind me coming to a stop. Here it was my engineer friend Jim. He was bringing me hot tea and several breakfast burritos. I grabbed the tea just to warm my hands.

I thanked him and told him I was okay, but I guess he noticed my flimsy gloves, because the next morning, now 30 miles or more from Sanderson, he found me again on the road, brought tea and burritos again, and also brought a great pair of bright orange railroad worker's gloves. They were about a thousand times better than my cotton ones. I just felt such profound gratitude. I'll never forget people like Jim and Sandra, generous both materially and personally.

But maybe the most lasting gift he gave me was that he told his Union Pacific engineer buddies about me. I guess I was pretty recognizable out there along the road with my cart, my dog and that orange hat, because it seemed the engineers often spotted me walking or even saw my tent along the railroad, and when they saw me, many times they'd give a quick couple toots on the locomotive horn to say hello. I knew they wished me well. I needed that. Those engineers were on the same journey as I was, I just wasn't carrying as much weight. I heard their friendly greetings all the way to California.

CHAPTER 16

The Wild West
Mid-February

Blog entry February 4: *The distances out here, like I said, are pretty enormous sometimes. It's really very open country and the thing that I've noticed the most is that except for the noise of the traffic which occasionally goes by, the only sound that I hear most of the time is the wheels of my cart rolling along on the pavement. The sound is occasionally broken by the croak of a raven or the rattling call of cactus wren but other than that it's pretty quiet.*

I walked the rest of the way to Marathon, Texas. Marathon is one of those western towns that's like an island. Coming from the east, I'd just walked 54 miles with no services of any kind, carrying the food and water for three days and two nights after leaving Sanderson. Sanderson, I guess, was like an island also. These towns are surrounded by the harsh but beautiful West Texas desert, not entirely flat but mostly barren.

Recently the whole area, all 500 miles from San Antonio to El Paso, has been savaged by drought conditions. I could no longer count on Xena getting her drinking water from puddles. There were no puddles. There hadn't been any real rain. The lack of water seemed to have taken its toll on the wildlife. All through West Texas I neither saw nor heard any coyotes, saw no jackrabbits or mammals of any kind and only a few birds. It was unsettling. It was just too quiet. It wasn't that I was on the interstate or anything which might have kept them from view. No, I had left San Antonio on Route 90 well south of I-10 and followed it all the way to Van Horn. (It did eventually join the interstate there and I-10 became the only road to El Paso.)

But animals or not, Route 90 is beautiful in a western desert kind of way, with endless vistas of the western rolling landscape. It was out there that I realized the difference between the mountains in the West and those further east. The western mountains are younger and so are visibly jagged, having little or no vegetation along their ridges. The mountains seem to rise up out of an otherwise flat plain. Naturally all western roads are built across these wide, flat plains. Eastern mountains, on the other hand, are heavily forested and their ridges have a soft fuzzy appearance. Also they don't rise out of flat plains, but rather are part of an overall blanket of undulating earth. When driving back east, one mountain obscures the next and so on, and the roads, by necessity travel up and down through the endless folds of those blankets.

Out west, very little is obscured at all. The traveler senses that he can see more of the "big picture." Even though I had driven through this area before, I was overwhelmed by its sheer size and by its arid climate.

It was still winter. As I came toward Marathon, I was cold in the mornings and chilly at night, so when my son Isaac told me there was a couch-surfing host in Marathon, I looked forward to some warmth. I got the call from a woman named Ingrid. She invited me to stay there at an address in town. I came into the town from the east, of course. The first intersection was with the road going south to Big Bend National Park, a hundred miles away. I knew that road well and would have loved to visit Big Bend again, but this time I was headed only straight west. No time for sightseeing or birdwatching side trips.

I stopped right there at the first gas station/cafe for a rest and a sandwich, then headed to "downtown" Marathon. A few blocks farther, I found a small grocery. I got some supplies and asked for specific directions to Ingrid's. The store lady knew exactly where it was and told me that it was at the end of 6th Street, that I couldn't miss it. I could tell that something was going to be different about this stopover. As I headed down 6th Street, I started seeing some unusual looking buildings on the last property. Most of Marathon was made up of ranch-type houses in various states of care and fanciness. Ingrid's place looked like it was handmade. It was.

Most of the buildings on her property are made of a mixture of cement and paper. The mixture hardens over a wood and wire frame. Some of the structures were neat and square, some had stone work as well. One small building, about the size of a Volkswagen, looked like a giant pterodactyl had dropped an eight-foot egg onto the landscape. It had one small door, one window and a small concrete bed platform. Can you guess where I would spend my time there? That's right, I would spend four nights in that egg.

Ingrid welcomed me to stay and introduced me to several other folks who were either visiting or had lived there a while. Ingrid hailed from the Czech Republic and spoke perfect English, but with a strong accent. She was in charge of this conclave. Her husband, who was in India at the time, had been the founder of this colony; they spoke on the phone daily. Ingrid gave me a small space heater for the egg house and I spent the first night plenty warm. The next day the weather forecast concerned me. I went to Ingrid. I told her the forecast showed some strong wind and some rain for the next three days. I had 30 miles to walk to Alpine, the next town. Ingrid said I could stay as long as I wanted and she meant it. I was very grateful and decided to wait out the weather.

That same morning I went back to see her. I told her that if I was going to be there two or three days, I needed a project. She knew that I had been a housepainter and so enthusiastically suggested that I might be able to complete a project she'd been needing done for three months. I was to spend the next three days turning an 8'x11' storage room with no interior walls (just bare studs) into a large walk-in closet. I could see it was a dream for her to have some major closet space. We drove to Alpine for some materials, came back and I started right in putting up walls, trimming out the whole room, painting it and putting up three room-length closet rods. It kept me very busy for three days and more than repaid my obligation to Ingrid. The moment I showed her the finished room, she ran to get a beautiful dress on a hanger and delightedly hung it on the newly installed rods. We were both very happy.

Ironically the weather each day there turned out to have been okay for walking. Each day I'd think, "I should have been walking today," but I enjoyed the break. I put my mind to a completely different task those three days and I got to meet some other travelers—bicyclists, who were also on long cross-country trips. Ingrid's place was well-known.

Refreshed in mind and body, I finally took off for Alpine. Marathon is one town and Ingrid's is one place that I want to visit my next time through. Driving, that is.

I almost forgot. Ingrid made a keen observation about where we were all living out there. She said that the whole western part of the state wasn't really Texas. Texas was Dallas and Austin and Houston and San Antonio. Where we were, there in that desert, was actually not Texas, but, as she called it, the "Wild West." As I pushed farther west I became more and more aware of this change, of this distinction. How different the landscape and the towns were. How much wilder the West had become!

CHAPTER 17

The Rest of Texas ✦ Marathon to El Paso
Late February

Blog entry February 10: *Anyway, the water report and the Xena report go together this time because when I give Xena water in her bowl I never waste the water, so by pouring the water back in to a particular coke bottle, which is different than my water bottles I can save it to give to her the next time. Well, you can imagine, yeah I have made a mistake a couple of times, and I have drunk water right out of the coke bottle after I've given her some. I've been drinking dog water, yuck! But she eats a lot of bones alongside the road, there's a lot of carcasses out here, so I assume her mouth is pretty clean. Anyway, you can tell I'm suffering!*

I left Marathon for the two-day walk to Alpine. This is beautiful country, winding uphill all the way past Alpine to Marfa. The incline is noticeable to a walker but it's not mountain-climbing. A steady push was sufficient. Mechanically, I was moving at a good pace, higher and further west every day. I made it to Alpine just fine and then heard from Greg and Lily Wilson, couch-surf hosts in Marfa. The weather was deteriorating to a cold heavy mist, so I was grateful when Lily picked me up at a convenience store and took me to their home. That rainy night we shared a great take-out pizza. The next day was so chilly and miserable that I gratefully stayed over another night. By the way, if you ever go through Marfa, go to the east end of town early at night; there you can hope to see the "Marfa Lights." These are an unexplained phenomenon of balls of light that appear almost every night. The origin of these lights is truly a mystery—look them up on the Internet! No one has ever trapped them, tracked them down or made any explanation of their source. This has been going on for over a hundred years, well before electricity, car lights, air traffic or any other modern wizardry. I'll go back to Marfa again soon I hope, to see these moving balls of light for myself.

I left Marfa the next day; any traveler would be sure to notice the simple sign along the road which says, "No Services Next 74 Miles." For most people this means turn around and get some gas in Marfa if you need it. For me it meant four days of walking before money would do me any good! When they say "no services," they mean exactly that. In that stretch, there is not a single place to buy anything to eat or drink, not even a soda machine, and no supplies of any kind.

Van Horn would be the town at the end of Route 90. There I would meet the interstate and its frontage roads to El Paso, at the western tip of Texas. Making it to Van Horn became my biggest challenge yet on the walk. It would be the longest and most desolate mileage of the trip, similar but more extreme than even the highway challenges I had navigated after Del Rio. It was only because I had already been through so much that I had the determination to push on.

The first two days out of Marfa took me to the only break in that 74 miles, the small village of Valentine. The folks in Valentine have a small post office and, surprisingly, a beautiful small library. Of course I visited both of these since there was nothing else in town. The library is in what was once a private southwestern style home. It's stocked with a large number of books, all neatly arranged on perfect shelving in two attractive, cozy rooms. I was glad to find it open. The lady in charge welcomed me, telling me that the library had been started as an endowment from one man, and was now maintained by town volunteers. I rested there and read through some historical books before going outside to fill my water jug from their hose. I then headed down to the post office, where I chatted briefly with the lady in charge. I told her that she should start a convenience store. She would be the only vendor for 35 miles in either direction!

Two more days walking finally found me close to the much larger town of Van Horn. Late in the afternoon, I had to decide whether to camp under a small bridge three miles from town or try to make it to whatever came first in Van Horn. As I stood at that bridge in the gathering dusk, a border patrol agent drove by and saw me. His name was David. He pulled up next to me to see if I needed help. I told him that although I could see the lights of the town, I couldn't tell how far it was. I added that I had already walked 20 miles that day. He could see I was tired. He then surprised me by volunteering to drive to town, measure the mileage and come back to tell me. What would take me two hours to do, he did in six minutes! He came back and confirmed that it was just over three miles. I decided to walk even though it would be dark long before I arrived. I really wanted to get some hot food and maybe stay in a warm motel that night.

The first place of business in Van Horn was a truck stop. After a cappuccino, I called the Motel 6 and got directions. The motel was almost another three miles on the west side of town. Motel 6 allows dogs. I walked the three miles for a total of 26 miles that day, the most I would do on the entire trip. I was assigned a room and went to it, only to find it already occupied by a rather startled older woman. The office got me another room and soon I was asleep; I was exhausted but ecstatic that I had conquered Route 90. California seemed, and actually *was*, closer than ever.

Blog entry February 15: *Here is where my trip takes on the new type of challenge. After 1500 miles I now begin walking the interstates, or more exactly, the frontage roads along the interstate, if there are any. The real challenge or fear now is that state troopers will stop me on the sections of interstate where there are no frontage roads. I keep playing over in my head what I'll say to them, but it's basically "What else can I do?" There are no secondary roads as an alternative. I'm worried about it, but between my mission and all, I'm hoping they'll be tolerant. I guess I'll find out!*

From Van Horn, it was mostly frontage roads along I-10 all the way to El Paso. (Frontage roads are roads which run very close and parallel to a superhighway, are usually paved, not overly wide, and provide access mostly for local traffic between exits.) At one frontage road exit, an SUV stopped when its driver saw my sign. In the SUV were a young couple, John and Makela Holecek and their daughter, Ruth. They were from San Diego! They had stopped because John had walked the Pacific Crest Trail, which runs from San Diego to the Canadian border, so I suppose John saw me as a hiking comrade. As we stood and talked, John described his walk, which was almost as many miles as I would walk, the difference being that many people walk the trail each year at the same general time so solitude is not the same as it was for me.

John and Makela asked me if I had picked a particular place to get to the ocean in San Diego. I told them I had seen a place on the north central shore called Ocean Beach. They laughed and said that they could look down from their hillside home and see that very beach. They gave me some water and cheese and told me that when I'd get to San Diego (they said "when!") I could call them about a place to stay. You can bet I wrote that number down and didn't lose it!

Some of the frontage roads in that area weren't like the typical ones that closely hug the interstate. Out in this area they seemed to be more like side roads which arced well away from the main highway. I found myself south of the interstate, practically along the Mexican border, with the tree line along the Rio Grande well in sight. I felt pretty vulnerable but could only push on. I kept a sharp eye for any movement anywhere out on the desert landscape. I saw none. Through the towns of Sierra Blanca and Fort Hancock I walked, camping three more nights and staying in one motel. I got a call from another couch-surfing host, Russ Koch in El Paso. He knew an Audubon man, John Sproul, who had a pickup and could get me to Russ' home in west El Paso. I was grateful to get into John's truck. I knew it meant that I was just about through Texas.

As we drove to Russ' house, John told me about the extensive work he was doing daily as an Audubon volunteer. The project involved trying to restore the wetlands in a threatened area east of El Paso. It reminded me that although I was getting some publicity for my walk, the real workers for the environment were out there every day working physically, mentally, and legally to protect what we have. They get a lot less press than I've gotten. They keep doing it.

It was a fun visit with Russ; he had hosted many couch-surfers and always enjoyed playing the piano for them. We went out for dinner and I came home to a good night's sleep. Before retiring for the night, Russ gave me accurate directions on the best road to take heading north to Las Cruces. I was still in El Paso and needed that help in navigating the still rather urban landscape. Russ left for work early the next morning. I left him a thank you note and walked out his driveway. I found the back road which went north up into New Mexico. Twenty more miles and Texas would be history.

Others Along the Way
West Texas

-Jerry and Max at the book store in Alpine, generous.
-Erin, a game warden who stopped along the road.
-John Pearson from Massachusetts at the picnic area, generous.
-Rudy and Nuny with FedEx, both stopped along the road.
-Maria at the Valentine post office.
-Eli, the counter man at the Motel 6 in Van Horn.
-Nice young waiter and the owner at Michael's Restaurant in Sierra Blanca. A free meal!
-M. Calanche, a border patrol agent at mile marker 99.
-Justin at the Fort Hancock mercantile.
-The owner at the Arzate Grocery in Fort Hancock.
-Edie Cenazeros, generous.

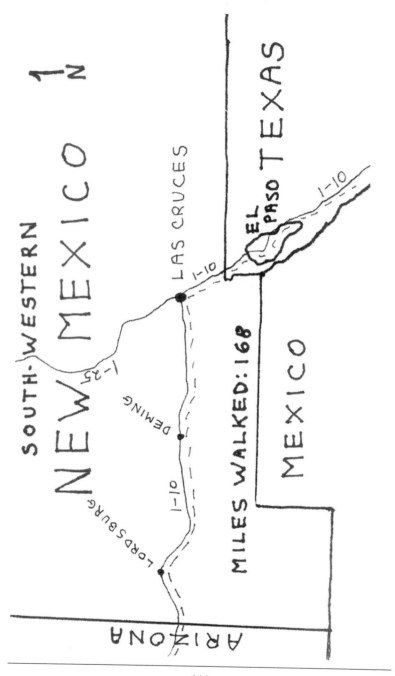

SOUTH-WESTERN
NEW MEXICO
N ↑

ARIZONA

LORDSBURG

I-10

DEMING

I-10

I-25

LAS CRUCES

I-10

EL PASO
TEXAS

I-10

MEXICO

MILES WALKED: 168

144

CHAPTER 18

New Mexico 🖋 The Horrible Wind
End of February—Early March

Blog entry March 1: *It's March 1st, I made it through February! It's been cold at night and my water froze again last night. I hope it will warm up again, at least a LITTLE and not too fast! I made 15 miles today even against the wind.*

Leaving El Paso I had about 20 miles to walk until I would be done with Texas. As I said, it had been over 800 miles across that state. I was finally going to be in New Mexico and it was only 168 miles more to reach Arizona. No other state had been such a short stretch. I thought it would be easy. It would turn out to be very punishing.

New Mexico was the only state where I didn't see a "Welcome to" sign. I had come up a back road from El Paso and didn't know the route that well, except that it headed toward Las Cruces.

I stopped at a church building of some kind and only realized I was no longer in Texas when I saw the letters "NM" on the church's electrical box by the road. I was so glad to have crossed all of Texas, that my blog for the day said simply, "New Mexico."

I made it up to my couch-surfing house in Las Cruces, where I was hosted by two great guys, Jim and Dean. Jim had travelled much throughout the world, Dean stayed home mostly. We shared a lot about my walk and their experiences.

In Las Cruces that same night, my son Brad and my 11-year-old grandson Nicolas drove down from Los Alamos to see me. They had a hotel room and the hotel had hot tubs. I left my couch-surf to visit with them. Soaking in the hot water, I knew that it was a rare treat and that most nights from then on I'd be back in my tent alone and not so comfortable.

The next morning at Jim and Dean's, my son came over and worked on my cart, readjusting the front wheel which had started to bend under the cart. I had had to make frequent stops to get it to track in a straight line. My son is an engineer at the national laboratory in Los Alamos, a nuclear facility, and seemed quite capable doing what was needed. I guess I could have done it, but I was pretty exhausted mentally and was grateful to just let him do it.

After goodbyes to my hosts and a breakfast with Brad and Nick, the boys took me out to the interstate to begin my trek across New Mexico. I can only wonder what my grandson thought, as a young man, watching his 66-year-old granddad start out that barren roadway.

It wasn't long before the wind started. I was of course walking west, and one thing you quickly learn is that generally the wind comes from that direction. It was still February. I wore a shirt, a thermal overshirt, a windbreaker and my heavy coat. On my head I wore two ski masks, one being a wind-resistant liner. My glasses protected my eyes. Xena needed no extra coat but had no eye protection. I don't know how she did it. She never complained.

I, however, complained a lot. Four out of five days going from Las Cruces to Lordsburg, I faced such punishing winds that I found myself gritting my teeth and literally gnashing them at that relentless torrent of air. It was at least twice as hard to walk as it would have been on a calm day. I had expected to enjoy New Mexico. I had lived in Albuquerque for two years and I love the Southwest, but walking against a 40-mile-an-hour gale was not my idea of fun at all. I hated it, but as with any adversary, I knew that I had to overcome it. Besides, I couldn't just sit there on the side of the road. I had to keep walking.

I took a break from the wind by staying at a motel in Deming. That night I got a call from my daughter telling me that my brother-in-law David was quite ill and was in the hospital. I decided to stay there a full day to await word on his condition. After a day's layover, the news was better. I decided that I could continue the walk, just staying in touch by phone. As I walked out of Deming that day, I decided to dedicate the rest of my walk to my brother-in-law. He and I had been Scoutmasters together and long-time friends. I realized that my struggles with the wind, the sand, the traffic—none of that compared with the struggle that he was experiencing. It gave me a new perspective which I would carry through whatever came my way.

Before I was out of New Mexico, however, I did make one mistake. I didn't pay close enough attention to what I had been told by a cross-country bicyclist. He had told me to cross over the highway at a certain exit where the frontage road continued along the north side instead of along the south side where I'd been walking.

When I got to that intersection, it seemed like the south frontage road was fine, so I didn't bother to cross over. I hadn't gone but about two miles when I saw a sign that grabbed my attention. It said simply, "Pavement Ends." Sure enough the paved road changed to packed clay and gravel. Soon, that walkable surface became barely walkable dirt, and the road veered somewhat away from the interstate. It seemed to continue to parallel the main highway so I kept going, not wanting to walk backwards for more than two miles. The dirt road became a farmer's field road. That small field road became a path and finally petered out altogether, leaving me with a view of open desert. I knew I was still heading west and my map showed another highway intersecting the interstate about two miles further on, so I began pushing my cart through the desert, over fairly hard-packed sand, steering around the mesquite and creosote bushes.

I couldn't have just gone at any point and crossed over the interstate. Barbed-wire barriers on both sides of the highway made that difficult. Of course there was also the danger of crossing four lanes and a median, so I was trying to stay safe. Until I was pushing there in that last stretch of desert, I had hoped I'd get through somehow without having to attempt a crossing other than at an exit. I finally saw that exit ahead on the horizon. As I approached the road coming in from my left, I came to the first barbed-wire fence. Those fences are to keep livestock off our highways. For me to cross, I had to unload my cart and put everything over the fence, climb over it and repack my cart. All that was just to get up onto the bridge that goes over the interstate.

Unfortunately, as I crossed that bridge, I then found that the bridge went over the highway all right, but there was no connection with the north frontage road, only with the on and off ramps for I-10. I had to clear another barbed-wire fence to access the north frontage road. Same process all over again.

All this was due to my not having taken in the important information from the biker. At times like this I could only laugh at myself. After all, I wasn't hurt and Xena was okay; I just felt sort of dumb.

Using I-10 and some more poor-condition frontage roads, I finally made it to Arizona. My seventh state welcomed me with a big sunny sign and the reminder that it was the Grand Canyon state. I knew I wouldn't be seeing the Grand Canyon this trip. I would stay well to the south, continuing along I-10. I figured the wind had to quit now that I was out of New Mexico. I was wrong; it kept blowing. Ominously, it was also warming up.

Others Along the Way
New Mexico

-Maria who stopped along the road and gave me directions!
-Amy at Boone Transportation.
-Maria at the Mesquite Mercantile.
-Dr. Vince, who stopped along the road, generous.
-The couple at Apache Homelands, generous.
-Juan of the border patrol.
-Dan the lineman.
-Kevin and Tom at the Deming exit Chevron.
-The young couple who mailed that important letter for me!
-Raevon, gave me a bag of goodies.
-Jim at the Lordsburg truck stop.
-Mark at the Lordsburg grocery.

-The Esserly family selling Girl Scout cookies at the Love's in Lordsburg. They gave me a free box of cookies!

-Laurie at the Love's, generous.

-Jared at that same Love's.

-Jason, a man with quite a story, the host at the Road Forks Motel.

Saguaro

CHAPTER 19

Arizona 🕊 "It's Not My Problem!"
Still Early March

Blog entry March 4: *So last night, with the sun setting 15 miles in front of me, over the Chiricahua Mountains in Arizona, I put up my tent along the interstate, here in New Mexico, and went to bed grateful for a good day of walking. Xena is doing fine, very well behaved along the interstate. Troopers and sheriffs have just driven by, no hassle at all. 550 Miles to go. I've crossed the Continental Divide [just before the Arizona border]. That's the dividing line for all rainfall, where it either goes to the Atlantic Ocean or the Pacific Ocean. A big milestone!! Maybe it will be more downhill from here?*

Blog entry March 5: *Before noon. Arizona. Mile Marker 390. I stayed in a motel last night and am entering Arizona clean and well fed.*

The wind continued well into Arizona. I walked along the interstate through Bowie and Willcox and Benson, knowing that the city of Tucson was my next big urban obstacle. I was looking forward to Tucson. There is a very active Audubon chapter there and there were couch-surfing hosts as well. However, I was not prepared for what would come next around mile post 287.

As soon as I saw the flashing lights on top of the trooper's car, I knew it wasn't going to be just another day. I had been walking along the I-10 in Arizona for over a hundred miles hoping that the "No Pedestrian" signs applied to everyone else but me. I had my excuses all prepared. First: bicycles are allowed, why not me? Second: There are no frontage roads, where am I supposed to walk? Third: (throwing myself on his mercy) I'm walking across the United States and a guy did it last year and didn't get stopped. Can't I just walk to the next frontage road? I'm friendly and, uh...

I don't know if I got all those excuses out before the trooper, Officer Rael, made it clear. Nothing was going to work. His response: "It's not my problem. But you may NOT walk on our interstate. Last year's guy was just lucky not to get stopped. Yes, we allow bicycles but not pedestrians." When I asked what I was supposed to do, he simply said "I can call you a cab," which he did. He made it clear that the only alternative was to arrest me. I opted for the cab.

For the next 45 minutes, waiting for the cab, the trooper and I discussed all kinds of topics: my walk, police work, world problems. He was a great state trooper, friendly and helpful but definitely by-the-book. The cab finally arrived and we loaded my cart, my dog and me into it for the 17-mile trip to the next frontage road. I said goodbye to the cop and thanked him. After all he had been very professional and had given me a great souvenir, suitable for framing: an official warning stating the charge of "criminal trespass." More importantly I knew that he and whatever passing motorist had called me in to him, had saved me the agony of walking any farther on the interstate.

Interstates are nerve-wracking. Although they almost always have a fairly wide (five feet or so) paved berm along the side, traffic was sporadically very intense, with multiple semis passing each other at 75 or 80 miles an hour. All this would be within five feet of my cart. I'd be pushing and steering with one hand, and the other controlling Xena on a shorter than usual leash.

As I rode in the taxi, I knew it would be difficult keeping my word to the trooper, but I also knew that now I'd have a new and better challenge. Avoiding the interstate would surely lead me to more interesting paths through Arizona. That turned out to be more than true.

I paid my 42 dollars to the cab driver, reassembled my cart on the side of the frontage road and headed for Tucson. The frontage road merged into a small highway leading into the heart of Tucson. Soon I was on sidewalks and crossing at traffic lights.

Looking back, I have to say that my experience with the trooper and the cab had actually been perfect. It was also in direct contrast to the experience that Anthony, last year's walker, had had in California. He had told me that he wasn't expecting the California Highway Patrol to stop him along the southern interstate, or anywhere. After all, he had walked on interstates in Texas, New Mexico and Arizona with absolutely no hassle.

So it was a great surprise to Anthony when the California troopers stopped him, questioned him, frisked him, checked his identification, and then took all his belongings, cart and all, and *threw* everything over the barbed-wire fence that runs along the interstate. They told him to get off, right then and there, get off the highway property. He described them as mean. It had sounded mean to me. (After hearing his tale, I had already decided not to do it in California but thought Arizona would be okay.) Anthony had to call a friend from Yuma to come get him and drive him to a frontage road farther west.

I knew that with only Arizona and California before me, that I had walked my last interstate stretch. I would have to adapt and adjust through the most challenging terrain of my entire walk. It would be mostly pure Sonoran Desert, and now it was getting seriously hot and continued warming more every day.

Others Along the Way
Eastern Arizona

-Charley the UPS driver and the other nice people at Dwayne's.
-Rae, the Bowie Fire Chief, generous.
- And then there was Ruth Romo, a couch-surfer from El Paso who saw me along the road and recognized me from my online profile. She stopped and helped me on an impossibly windy day (40-60 mph winds!).
-Mickey and Mike at the Bowlin's store.
-Brian Whitaker and his son Brian, Jr., at the Arizona rest area.
-Rick at the "CG" motel in Benson; he had no rooms open but found a place for me to sleep in an empty van!
-Dennis and Shevanne Krump, Mark and the girls, Brian and Lydia and the girls, and Vera and Judith, all at the Wal-Mart in Benson.

-And then there was Jesus Christ, which was the only name given to me by an unusual and thoughtful man I met at a shady picnic table outside a convenience store. We each had something to eat and we talked about salvation, the government, and how much needs to be done!

-Rachel, a very interesting older lady with a cart and a collection of troll dolls.

Campbell Auer meets Xena.

CHAPTER 20

Tucson to Yuma
March 10-29

Ever since San Antonio, the desert had presented an entirely different kind of challenge. This was due to the lack of trees and bushes and to the distance between towns. Another challenge was coming on gradually and added a new dimension to my difficulties. This new challenge was the increasing heat.

Since Georgia and Alabama, I had either been walking in mild days or cold days. In the cold, you can bundle up and tough it out; in the heat you have to stop when it gets too intense. The heat didn't really become an issue again until Arizona; now in March the days became more like they had been back East. I was walking a lot in the morning and resting some during the heat of the afternoon. I would hang out at a convenience store for hours if necessary, until the afternoon would cool down a bit. Between stores, there was little shade. An overpass or a large concrete culvert under the road was sometimes all I could find.

Now, as I walked into the eastern side of Tucson late in the afternoon, the days were still pretty tolerable. I followed the city streets until I came to a hotel in center city. There I had arranged to attend a monthly meeting of Tucson Audubon. I arrived at 6:30, barely a half hour before the meeting started. I was introduced at the beginning so that I might briefly tell the members about my walk for Audubon. I got a pretty good laugh from them when I told them about several people I had met along the route who thought that Audubon actually was the Autobahn in Germany. Many of those people had asked me why I was walking to support that high-speed highway in Europe!

That night I couch-surfed with Ron Dahlin, who picked me up at the hotel after the meeting. Back at his home, we had one of those great conversations where each person takes turns talking, then listening. Ron gave me a great place to sleep and dropped me the next morning at the staff offices of Tucson Audubon near the western edge of town. Their offices are in a beautiful desert setting with saguaros and ocotillos all throughout the walking trails around the building. The head honcho there, Paul Green, shared with me his long history of environmental work, and the legal battles and compromises that they face on a daily basis. He was well aware of the work of the other Audubon offices, such as those on the Gulf Coast and in Baton Rouge, Houston and San Antonio. It was encouraging to hear that Audubon was connected in these ways throughout America.

I left with the staff's good wishes and headed down the road toward the long frontage road that went west to the next big town, Casa Grande, 75 miles away. The railroad was still with me, still pushing west to Yuma and north to Phoenix. Each day I camped as late as possible so that darkness would give me extra cover. With few bushes to hide in, setting up my tent in daylight felt like I was putting myself on exhibit. One night I camped behind a huge, graffiti-covered wall at an exit in Red Rock. The train tracks were about 50 feet away. I was more exposed there than ever before and I remember feeling like, "Oh, well. If anyone other than the train engineers see me, I'll just have to deal with it!" No one seemed to notice and I made it on through Red Rock and Eloy and then into Casa Grande.

In Casa Grande I had an old friend, Campbell Auer. I had met him about 10 years before when my van blew an engine in that town. He had given me some work while I waited 10 days for my van to be repaired. Campbell is an unusual artist and craftsman, having developed a technique for applying a sand finish, complete with figures and symbols of authentic Southwestern art, onto electrical switch and outlet covers. His company is called GEOPLATE. He travels to craft shows and sells over the Internet.

Campbell hosted me for three days of rainy weather. During that time he helped me get the busted zipper on my tent replaced (I was getting a little paranoid about scorpions getting in with me at night). He introduced me to his helper, Dan, his good friend Marge and to his brother Jim. We all had a great time sharing our life stories. Marge had contacted the local press and arranged for Bill Coates, the editor of the Casa Grande Dispatch, to interview me. Bill wrote probably the best article about my trip. I couldn't have had a better time resting and visiting with Campbell, a true artist and a true friend. As soon as the weather cleared, however, I had to get going again.

Interstate 8 (I-8) splits off from I-10 in Casa Grande. While I-10 heads up toward Phoenix, I-8 goes more southwesterly to Gila Bend and Yuma. I-8 was therefore a better option for me since I wanted to avoid the huge urban area of Phoenix and also to stay all the way south through California to San Diego. Since there was no frontage road along I-8 toward Gila Bend, I had to head north from Casa Grande on the back road to Maricopa and then west down to Gila Bend.

Maricopa wasn't too far and had great stores, ice cream and more, but the distance from there to Gila Bend was much greater and very little travelled. Most of that stretch ran through the Sonoran Desert National Monument. My days began to blur together; just adding miles was becoming quite mechanical. I told myself I was a walking machine. After any rest, I'd get up and start again, usually stiff in the legs from sitting. I'd start chugging, like a train coming out of the station, and after a hundred yards or so, I'd be cruising again at top speed, three miles an hour. Robotically, I'd tack on the miles and tens of miles. I still had over 300 miles to go and it was all desert. Two more nights camping brought me into Gila Bend, which I knew was the last outpost of any size until Yuma, still over a hundred miles away, at the California border.

Blog entry March 24: *Arizona has been tough. The wind was bad in New Mexico and continued to Tucson. Gusts up to 60 miles per hour...Now I'm in Gila Bend, with one 100 mile stretch of back road to Yuma on the California border. I just went through the beautiful Sonoran Desert National Monument area. A 40 mile stretch, of saguaro and mountains. Very quiet with no trains or traffic. Ahead are concerns with heat, with border issues and urban areas, rattlesnakes and scorpions, [which in the Southwest can be lethal, unlike their Southeastern cousins] and centipedes are out there. But at least at night they can't get through the new zipper in my tent. I don't know if mountain lions may be a factor when I go through the desert state forests in California. I'll get some info on that, I guess. Thank goodness, Xena would warn me at least. It's not far now, 320 more miles.*

I arrived in Gila Bend late in the day and started looking for a motel. As I crossed a street in town, I struck the front wheel of my cart on a curb, breaking the wheel from its mounting on the frame. It wasn't just loose, it was definitely broken. I was horrified. I knew I'd be stuck in Gila Bend until somehow I repaired it. I went ahead and got a motel room and spent the night trying not to worry about what I would do the next day. In the morning I set out to find a hardware store. At a well-stocked resale store, a helpful guy named Art gave me some good advice and some possible parts, but it wasn't until I met Eric Johnson in front of the only hardware store that progress was made. Eric got tools from his truck. Together, but mostly due to his expert advice and hard work, we actually got the wheel back on. I had dodged a bullet again and now felt confident that the wheel was stronger than ever. I knew that it could definitely make it to the Pacific!

The desert plants all became as familiar to me as the cotton and blueberries had been back in Georgia. The prickly pear, the saguaro, the ocotillo, the yucca, the mesquite and creosote bushes and the sage were all around with mostly just sand in between. Comfort at night was not really a problem with all that sand, but the cactus spines had to be avoided. Several nights I camped well off the road among the saguaros. Those are the huge cylindrical cactuses that grow "arms." Everyone warned me about rattlesnakes. Because of that, I never walked after dark because that's when snakes would come out to lie on the warm roads. Surprisingly, I never saw any live snakes, night or day, on the whole walk. I thought surely Xena would get bitten by a campsite intruder at night or even just along the road. I guess she lucked out, but the danger was there.

After Gila Bend, there's about a 20-mile stretch of frontage road along I-8, but then it quits. A good Arizona map showed a small road that heads north from that point for about 15 miles, then it turns west and south, eventually working its way for over a hundred miles into the agribusiness "suburbs" just east of Yuma.

This back road was my only option for crossing the rest of Arizona. Most maps show that the road goes only to the Painted Rock Dam, but a detailed map indicated there was a small road, a connection from that point to reach another road leading to the town of Hyder. I had been told, reliably, that there was a store in Hyder.

And so I headed up that first road going 20 miles or so from the "civilized" area around the interstate. I found myself that first night on a long stretch of road going through an area clearly posted as belonging to the Tohono O'odham Nation Indian Reservation. Having been through much of the Southwest before, I knew that the reservation police are very strict. I had no choice, however. I had to camp somewhere. Both sides of the road were signed as reservation land and showed no sign of coming to an end any time soon. I finally realized I'd have to hide well off this road and hope no one discovered us. I think during the whole night maybe only two pickups travelled that road. I slept well, got up and got quickly back on the road.

That morning I continued north through the Painted Rock Mountains. I skipped a visit to the dam because the connecting road I needed split off before the dam. I soon realized that this new little road wasn't on most maps because it was hardly a road for vehicles. It has an eight-mile section which consists only of heavy stones, much larger than regular gravel. I guess you'd be okay with a four-wheel drive, high clearance vehicle, but pushing a cart was tough. The wheels of my cart would dig into the stones. It was especially hard for the smaller front wheel, so I found myself tilting the cart backwards, lifting that wheel out of the stones altogether. Balancing, pushing and walking with Xena, that stretch was like no other. Amazingly, it was along this rough road that a number of hang-gliders were doing their thing from the high cliffs of the mountainside just north of me. They seemed to be enjoying themselves, drifting effortlessly on the desert winds. I wonder if they thought I was also having fun.

After about four hours, that section of road finally ended as it became once more a "normal" desert road of hard-packed sandy soil. To me, it seemed like I was back on a superhighway. I was again heading straight north. In the very far distance, maybe two miles, I could see what seemed to be a long, stationary railroad train. It seemed to stretch before me from as far as I could see to my right to as far as I could see to my left. I wondered how I would get past this blockade but I could only keep walking toward it. As I drew closer, I finally could see that my road came to a "T" just before the train and that my path took a sharp left turn right there. I knew then that I wouldn't have to wait for the train to move or to try to cross somehow between cars or find my way around it. It was now just an interesting decoration along my walk as I made my way west.

I say it was decoration because many of the cars were artfully spray-painted with graffiti. Most of the artists, I suppose, were members of city gangs, and some of their work was really good, everything from "Peanuts" characters to bizarre space alien figures forming odd gang-related names or messages. Some examples (of the ones that weren't so artistically distorted that you couldn't figure them out) were SUM SORROW, BABES, METH, RESET, SIZE 21, VOTE, and PORK. All were done in brilliant colors, their letters interwoven and compacted almost or usually to the point of being unreadable; the fact that they were unreadable did not, however, in any way detract from their art.

At this point, I still had six miles to go to Hyder. The motionless train was on my right for over two of those miles. I figured there were over 500 cars on that train. I guess those cars either weren't operable or were in some sort of limbo. They just sat there, seemingly abandoned in the desert.

The road had become monotonously uniform. It was mostly only wide enough for one car, hemmed in often on both sides by small sandy embankments which provided a steady influx of sand onto the road surface. That sand created problems for me whenever the road would drop down into even a small dip. In those spots, there would be a bed of sand covering the whole road and stretching for a hundred feet or more. Pushing through those sand drifts required me to bend over with my arms straight in front and to dig in with each step. I would veer from right to left and back again, hoping to track the part of the road with the least sand. I felt like a fish swimming along looking for the best current. I suppose that was ironic because there was absolutely no water anywhere, just sand and bushes. Here and there there'd be a stand of salt cedar trees, 10 or 20 feet high with soft needles. At these I would stop for shade and for a chance to sit on their beds of fallen needles—anything for a change from the ever-present sand. I knew I wouldn't get to Hyder that day so I had to find somewhere to camp along that stretch of road. I had seen no traffic at all, not one car or truck all day. Still I sought to be out of sight from the road. I went several hundred feet off the left side of the road, out along a small gully, and found a spot among some bushes. I could still see the train just across the road. I was glad it was there.

Alone in the desert, the train cars represented at least something that was familiar, seeming to stand guard in an otherwise barren landscape. I was totally alone (except, of course, for Xena) farther from civilization than at any other point on my walk. I thought back to Trooper Rael in eastern Arizona and realized that this gift I had been given was due directly to his dutiful lack of pity. What luck! My adventure had been magnificently enhanced. Thank goodness my silly excuses had not worked on him. I was where I needed to be. I was where I wanted to be. I slept soundly.

Making it to Hyder the next morning was a pleasant surprise. A friendly couple, John and Charlotte Tryon, welcomed me to their small but well-stocked "convenience" store. I had been prepared for that store to be closed for any number of unforeseen reasons. I hadn't let myself do more than just sort of hope it would be open because any further dependence on it would have been devastating to me psychologically if it had been closed. But there I was, sitting with a cold Coke and an ice cream sandwich, right there in the middle of the desert. That store, Hyder Valley Supply, is the only source of food or supplies for 30 miles in any direction; anyone who has any business at all in that area of Arizona knows it's there. John and Charlotte told me that the next town on my map wasn't really there anymore. It was just what was left of an old railroad stop. It used to be that the railroads had to establish a stop about every 15 miles for water for the steam engines, but that need no longer existed, so the stops disappeared. The next store would be 30 miles west in the small town of Roll in the heart of the agribusiness area, many miles east of Yuma.

I headed out refreshed and continued along the desert road, past the turn south to Dateland, a town located on I-8. I knew that there were stores in Dateland but no frontage road. I had no choice but to stay straight west. I was still 70 miles from a town of any size.

I met a couple out there in a well-outfitted camper. They were Jim and Wendy Pearson and they were on a global trek, intending on heading south through Mexico, Central America and South America. They gave me a cold drink and some shade alongside their big vehicle. The challenges ahead for them were quite different from my challenges. We wished each other well and went in opposite directions. They were in the early stages of their trip and heading into different countries and cultures. Their progress and obstacles would be mostly vehicle related. In contrast, I was nearing the end of my trip and was staying in America. Any obstacles for me would not involve finding gasoline or water pumps or tires.

I found what was left of that "town" shown on my map west of Hyder. All that was there was a small stone foundation among the salt cedars. It was cool under those trees, at least cooler than the alternative! After another night in the desert, I made it to the little convenience store in Roll. After refreshment there, I took off for the 20 or 30 miles wending the way through the grid of roads separating the huge agricultural fields of wheat and various vegetables grown in the irrigated Arizona desert. Eventually, I came out to the town of Ligurta. Here there was a real problem. I had a couch-surf set up in Yuma but I was still 15 miles away. The problem was that there was no frontage road from Ligurta up and over the mountainous Gila Ridge.

So in Ligurta, I went into a small bar and restaurant at the interstate exit, right at the base of the mountain. I had a sandwich and a drink and talked with the bartender and two customers. They were interested in my trip and realizing my problem, one of the customers, John, said he had to drive up over that mountain to go home. He offered to take me over that narrow winding pass. It was just one of those times when I had to accept an offer of help. Not only had I promised the trooper to not walk on the interstate, it would have been dangerously foolish along that stretch. That road had no berm to speak of, and wound up and over the mountain pass; I would have been a danger to myself and others.

John let me out as soon as we cleared the mountain. I walked on toward Yuma until it was time to call my next couch-surfing host, James Delecki. A young active-duty army man, James came and picked me up in east Yuma. He gave me a place to stay and graciously, even though he had a rock-climbing outing to get to, drove me west the next morning, to the first frontage road just across the state line into California. I was done with Arizona. I was not, however, anywhere near done with the desert.

ΦΜΦ

Others Along the Way
Western Arizona

-Eric, on the sidewalk in Tucson, walking a dog almost identical to Xena.
-Martha at the Audubon meeting in Tucson, who took the time to talk to me about my walk.

-Mary at the K-Store in West Tucson.

-Al the biker, took our picture.

-Mary at the K-Store in Marana, a tough young woman who was hitchhiking.

-Adam the cross-country bicyclist. *I* took *his* picture!

-Dave Rodriguez, along the road near Casa Grande.

-Hortensia, the seamstress, who didn't charge me too much for replacing my tent zipper on a Sunday, even though she was getting ready for a big birthday party!

-Anthony and all the staff who like to sing while they work at the Maricopa Carl's Jr.

-Jennifer and her two daughters at that same Carl's Jr.

-And then there were Tim and Simeon, two EMTs at the Goodyear Fire Station west of Maricopa, in the middle of nowhere. They gave me a much needed place to sit inside, cool off, have a drink and talk. I left and got out to the road when they came running out to get our picture. They posed with my cart and I got their picture as well.

-Butch Roberts, an interesting guy travelling who stopped on the roadside ahead of me, then called to me as I approached. We talked for about 15 minutes. He had a revolver tucked into his belt.

-The nice ladies selling goodies and stuff at the Gila Bend Hardware.

-Misaella Montanez and his family at their home west of Gila Bend. I asked for water and the whole family hung out and talked about my trip while I rested. (Misaella was about 11 and the only one in his large family who spoke any English.) We all took pictures!

-Manuel at the farm irrigation discharge pipe.

-Christine, "the gypsy," along the road.

-Sherry at the Mohawk Valley School in Roll, who gave me directions and said she'd tell the kids about my walk.

-Loyd, the Ready Ice driver at Gonzo's convenience store in Roll.

-And then there was Madison Murdoch, a young farmer (18?) I met at Gonzo's in Roll. Further down the road, he came running out to give me 10 dollars in quarters for my walk. He said he'd been saving them for a new video game but wanted to give them to me. Amazing. I walked on, absolutely stunned. Why had a young man seen fit to give me his small savings like that? Probably no one else on my walk had been more generous. He gave me what he had.

-Jackie and her grandson Damien, on the road.

-Jim of the Yuma Sheriff's Department.

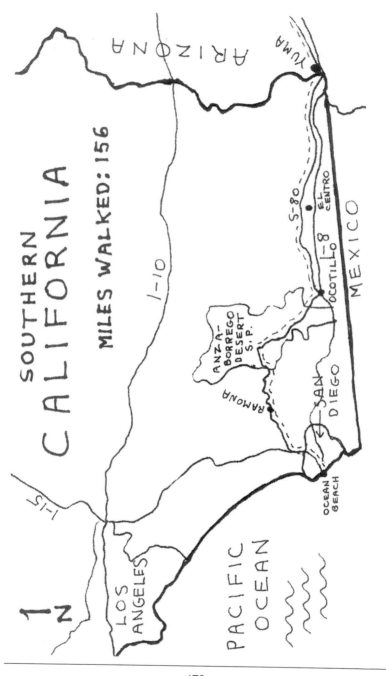

SOUTHERN
CALIFORNIA
MILES WALKED: 156

ARIZONA

I-10

I-15

YUMA

S-80

EL CENTRO

I-8

OCOTILLO

MEXICO

ANZA-BORREGO DESERT S.P.

RAMONA

SAN DIEGO

OCEAN BEACH

LOS ANGELES

PACIFIC OCEAN

N

CHAPTER 21

California ✒ The Home Stretch
March 30-April 6

Blog entry March 30: *Well, I have made it to California! I think I have made it through the heat. Arizona was very hot, had a lot of desert to walk through, and I am now in the desert of Southern California where two days ago, I had to spend the entire afternoon under a small bush with Xena because it was too hot for either of us to walk. I spread my rain poncho over the top of the bush for some shade and we lay there for four hours.*

Getting across the border into California deepened my belief that I would make it all the way; after all, there were now only about 150 miles to go. I realized it was possible, at the rate I had been walking, to make it to San Diego in little more than a week! This confidence had been gradually building, but now I was becoming pretty sure of that success. First, however, I'd be dealing with more frontage roads and desert all the way on through El Centro to Ocotillo. From Ocotillo I would go north up through more desert until I'd head west over the mountains.

Near Holtville, I came to a hot springs early in the day. I almost didn't interrupt my progress, but I'm glad I stopped. It was a welcome relief to first soak my feet then my whole body. How refreshing is hot water in a hot climate? Very. I met Jack and Pia there and enjoyed their company. Before I left, Jack gave me a Canadian "loony" (the equivalent of our dollar coin). Jack had been given the coin by Terry Fox, the man whose image appeared on the reverse of the coin. Terry Fox was an amputee who walked across Canada for the Cancer Society. Jack was leaving for Dallas in two days and I would love to have gotten a ride back to Texas with him, but I still had another week of walking. Refreshed by the hot springs and by the chance meeting, again I took off through the desert, heading for the sprawling desert city of El Centro.

I had only walked two days in California when I was helped by an overnight couch-surf there in El Centro, hosted by Rainy, a registered nurse with a dog-friendly home. Early the next morning, I made my way out of the city and started back into the desert. I still had two more days of walking on frontage roads to reach the small town of Ocotillo. Now I was averaging over 20 miles a day. The closer I was to the end, the more distance I tried to cover each day.

When I started the walk, back in Georgia, I had been happy with 12 miles a day. Gradually, as I got stronger and as the weather cooled off a bit, this number had crept up to where I was averaging 15 or 16 a day. On my last day getting back to Rob's house in Alabama, I had amazed myself by walking 19 or 20 miles. Of course, on that day I knew that there was a warm bath and a bed and my van at the end of the road, so I was highly motivated.

By the time I got to Arizona and California, I was pleased but not altogether surprised by making 20, 22 or 24 miles a day. After all, like I said, I was stronger and could now, without blistering my feet, walk for seven or eight of the 12 daylight hours. But there was something else at work also.

From one of my college classes, I remembered about the behavior of rats in a maze. It seems that once a rat has learned to run a maze, knowing he'll have a nice snack at the end of his run, he'll run it every time, faster and faster as he nears the end. The anticipation of the finish seems to create extra energy and desire to get his snack. As for me, just like those scurrying rodents, I could taste the reward that awaited me in the salty water of the Pacific. I found myself hurrying along, pushed by increasingly warm weather and by ever stronger legs. I was galloping to the finish! I was in the home stretch!

On April 1, I met a man named Smitty riding his bike along the road. He was the supervisor of a trucking company that had its terminal about 10 miles further on. He encouraged me to stop and camp there and I took him up on it. There were few places along this stretch of road that weren't private property so I made the effort to reach the terminal. This involved walking after dark, something I hardly ever had done. I made it at about 9 PM, camped alongside one of the big truck sheds, and heard truck loading sounds through most of the night. In the morning, I went to the office, found Smitty already hard at work and thanked him. Nothing exceptional had happened, it was just another of those many instances where someone made it possible for me to get through another night when I needed it the most.

That day, I stocked up in Ocotillo. It was there that I had to give up any further connection with I-8. There were no more frontage roads. I would now have to head north the 70 miles or so through the Anza-Borrego Desert State Park. This large expanse was pure Sonoran desert: long vistas of rugged Southwestern mountains and long stretches of flat valleys between those mountains; it was all cactus and other desert plants and sand—and one paved road. It was the most beautiful environment of my entire walk, but then I've always been partial to the Southwest. Not far inside the park boundary, I came to the S-2 Border Patrol checkpoint. The officers there welcomed me to sit and rest there as long as I wanted and gave me cold water. It was the heat of the day, so I stayed and talked with them for a couple of hours.

Coming across these deserts of Arizona and California, I had quite often taken time out from walking due to that afternoon heat. I mostly had to create my own shade by placing my rain poncho spread out over the largest creosote bush I could find. These bushes are the largest vegetation anywhere around, being about the size of an over-stuffed living room chair. Xena and I would lie down and back up under the suspended poncho, under and into the creosote bush. We would simply lie there like that for up to four hours waiting for the afternoon heat to subside. There were a few times when I felt a wave of panic sweep over me as I feared being overwhelmed by the heat. Two factors got me through the serious concern that gripped me. One factor was that I did have plenty of water and food. The other was that although traffic was scarce, there were some cars every so often. If something really was going wrong, like if Xena or I were feeling ill, I knew someone could be persuaded to stop. Out there in the desert, many people would respond to the dire need of a pedestrian and his dog.

Happily we didn't ever have to do that. After the border patrol stop, we camped for the night and made it the next day to a privately-owned resort, the Agua Caliente, complete with hot and cold water pools. I chose the hot pool. After refilling my water bottles, Xena and I headed out again along the paved park road.

Before I would be through the park, my map showed there was one mountain to climb, one long grade rising quickly over 1,000 feet. From far off, I could see it rising in front of me, the park road curling up to the top from left to right. The climb was so steep that I had to stop every 100 yards or so to catch my breath and even sit and rest. Bit by bit, I pushed the cart, bent forward, arms straight out, huffing and puffing. Reaching the top, I was exhilarated. I still had worries, but at least this long-dreaded obstacle was now behind me.

Camping each night wasn't too bad out there except I now had been introduced to a new concern: the possibility of mountain lions. At the only convenience store in the park, I sat and talked with two men, Fred and Trevor. They told me quite clearly about the presence of these cats in the park. They were usually found in the more tree-filled areas up the slopes of the mountains, but they were definitely around. Fred had lived right in those mountain areas for a long time and related the stories of the couple of times when a person had been taken by a lion. I had heard before of the one example, a woman birding alone. It was only maybe twice over a period of 10 years, but knowing the infrequency was hardly reassuring.

The lions were known to attack dogs. I knew that a hungry lion wouldn't think Xena was all that much too big to kill. As for me, I knew my tent offered no protection. I was very nervous, now less than a hundred miles from the Pacific surf.

At the north end of the park, the park road joins an east-west highway which goes west up and over the mountains and down to the coast. These mountains and the roads through them were my last obstacle. I asked about the road up to the summit town of Julian. I was told that it would be very unwise to try to walk it up to Julian or down the other side for another 10 miles or so. The road is narrow and curvy, snaking back and forth all the way to Ramona, very much like the mountain pass just east of Yuma.

It was getting dark as I approached that intersection, so I needed to make camp. Near that "T" intersection was a wooded area, the lower end of a forested slope along a small range of hills. To me it looked like mountain lion territory. Parked right at the intersection was one of those large yellow road-graders. I decided that rather than going over to the "protection" of those nearby trees, I'd put up my tent, right there, in the wind, beside and slightly underneath the cab of the grader. I did worry that someone might come along in the night to move the grader, starting it up and running over me before I could get out of the tent. Now that's a good example of a relatively irrational fear. I recognized it as such and decided that it was a less likely scenario than being eaten by a mountain lion. Some choice.

At dark, I was just about to tie my tent to the grader, when a car pulled up to the "T." I waved, they waved back. We looked at each other. I'm sure they were surprised to see a pedestrian out there, and while they were processing that surprise, like deciding to ask me what I was doing, I made a quick decision. I asked them if they were going up over the mountain. They said not really, but offered to take me anyway! My friends were Doug Vannier and his son Brandon. They helped me pack my cart into the back of their hatchback and Xena and I squeezed into the back seat. I left behind the mountain lions and the road-grader and we all started up the darkening road. The curves for the next 20 miles were severe. I can't imagine trying to walk such a stretch.

All the roads that go up over the mountains in Southern California, even the interstate, are winding and dangerous to walk. I watched from the back seat as the last of those curves went by, the small car's headlights sweeping back and forth until finally the road straightened out coming into Ramona. There the Vanniers took me to a campground, the Dos Picos. I spent my last night camping in the complete safety of that little park surrounded by happy vacationing campers, far from the worry of predators or the dangers of the mountain roads.

In the morning I was offered pancakes and coffee by a friendly family and then packed up and headed west. A couple of days before, I had called John and Makela (the couple I'd met in Texas who lived in San Diego). They were excited to hear from me and said again that I was welcome to stay with them. John said to call when I got close and he'd come get us in his pickup. Just north of San Diego, I came again to a short but dangerous set of curves, so I stopped, called John and waited there. Soon I was at their home, a lovely ranch house in the hills seven miles from the seaside town of Ocean Beach. The following morning was my last to walk. I would walk down to the beach and then back the seven miles to their house. I knew that those last fourteen miles would fly by.

I had worried and fantasized about one final problem which I was sure would arise. I could imagine that when I finally reached whatever beach I'd end up at, there'd be a big sign that read, "NO DOGS ALLOWED." For days I had created a scenario in my head whereby I would tell the law-and-order beach patrol person that Xena and I were going to walk that last hundred yards or whatever all the way to the water. After all, we'd come all the way from the ocean in Georgia together. We'd not quit until we'd both made it to the ocean in California! I was ready to tell them to go ahead and give me a citation if necessary. I'd pay whatever fine, but I knew we'd be getting all six feet wet!

Now that had been a noble fantasy, but it wasn't to be. The night before, John and Makela told me that none of that drama was going to take place because the road down to that particular spot in Ocean Beach empties right out onto what's known as Dog Beach! It's called that for one reason. Xena was one of about a hundred dogs on the beach that day. We put our bare feet in the welcoming surf and, except for walking back to the house, my walk was over.

There at the beach, I saw a nice young couple, Greg and Teresa, sharing a sweet kiss, right there near where we went in the water. I asked them if they'd mind taking our picture with my camera; I told them what we'd just accomplished. They were quite amazed and said they'd be honored, taking pictures of us with their own camera as well. None of my friends or relatives had been able to meet us there that day but I was fine with that. I'd just met a new couple. They would be my new friends and family for me in that singular moment. They were perfect.

Blog entry (Lucy's posting) April 6: *On the phone with dad RIGHT NOW...HE IS LOOKING AT THE WAVES OF THE PACIFIC!!!! They are at Dog Beach, in San Diego! 2,400 miles, seven months. I am so proud!*

Blog entry (Greg's posting) April 8: *My girlfriend and I were taking our dog "Chops" to the beach when Brad asked if we could take a picture for him and his dog as he had just walked across the country! I was super honored and lucky to be the one Brad met at the end of the road. I took a few pictures for him on his camera, but I had to get one for myself. What an awesome guy, with a great story. After reading his bio, I'm even more impressed. I spread the story as much as I could today, and will probably be talking about it forever. Thanks for getting it all online. It's a great read. -Greg*

Xena and I walked home to John and Makela's. We had a celebratory dinner and we went to bed—Xena in their beautiful, grassy, walled backyard, and me in a comfortable bed. Xena and I both slept soundly.

Others Along the Way
California

-Carlos and the Subway girls at the El Centro Shell.

-Josh and Jeff, on bicycles at the Seely store.

-The group of four-wheelers along the road. One of the dads had the kids all clap for me.

-Brian Clark on the road to Ocotillo. Told me a lot about his life.

-Kenny at the Ocotillo convenience store.

-Mike, Lauri and the boys out camping.

-John and Laura, volunteers at the Agua Caliente resort.

-Ryan, the ranger at the resort.

-June and Jeff and their seven grandkids, all camping!

-Heidi Trueblood and the kids at the Butterfield RV Park.

-Laurel and Paul, RVers who took me in in Anzo Borega and gave me orange juice, a sandwich and ice tea! They also told me that I was on the right road!

-Gregg on his bike and another man, Paul, at Dog Beach. They each asked about my trip. Smiling broadly and with wet feet, I told them!

CHAPTER 22

Having Made It, Now What?

Blog entry April 7: *We leave Monday in a crowded pickup truck to get back to San Antonio where my van is parked, so we can resume our "normal" lives! Xena has to ride in a carrier for the first time EVER in the back of the truck. I hope she doesn't think she is being jailed after completing this walk, instead of being carried home on a big satin pillow, like she deserves. I couldn't have done it without her.*

Finding myself at the Pacific Ocean in San Diego turned out to be a mixed blessing, as they say. I was overwhelmed, or at least, somewhat whelmed at having made it. Because I had been anticipating reaching my goal for at least several weeks, I wasn't surprised to be there. It didn't just happen like winning the lottery. I had seen it coming from miles away. Of course I was thrilled to have finished the walk. The other part of the "blessing" was the response I now had to make in answering that question posed to me by that little boy way back in Georgia, "What are you going to do when you get there?"

At the time, I answered that, by saying that I didn't know. I was pretty sure I wasn't going to walk back, and I knew I couldn't fly or take a bus with Xena. So my plans, as they had been for most of the trip, were to play it by ear. I still didn't know how I'd get back to San Antonio, back to my van, back to my normal life, my normal way of getting around.

My hosts, John and Makela, were not only kind and generous, they were also thoughtful. I don't think that it was just that they had to find a way to get me out of there (you know what they say about a guest after three days!) but they got creative for me. They went on Craigslist to look for possible rides going east.

The only response to their inquiry came with the possibility of chipping in for gas to a guy who was driving east all the way to Virginia—via Texas! I negotiated for a small reasonable sum and started packing. This fellow, Eric by name, was ready to leave the following morning and expected to have five riders, each of us to have a seat in his crew-cab pickup. I realized I'd have to put Xena in a doggie carrier and she'd have to ride in the bed of the truck along with everybody's packs and luggage. I didn't know how she'd do, riding like that, but she really didn't have much of a choice. This ride was it—the only ride available. My stay on the coast would be necessarily brief.

I had no dog carrier, of course, so Makela got online again and found one big enough for Xena being sold by a private owner not far away. We drove over, I bought it, and just like that, we were ready to go.

I had never given a lot of thought to the fact that my trip was planned to end in an urban area. If I had made it to that beach with no place to stay at night, can you imagine me then, turning on my sand-covered heels, looking east and muttering, "Oh. Now what?" But I had been lucky. Meeting John and Makela in Texas had led me here to their home where I had had four days of good times, good food, and plenty of rest. I was ready to leave, to endure a two-day, crammed-in ride.

The sun came up and here I was loading Xena in her carrier into the back of the pickup. I climbed in with three of the four other men and realized I'd be sitting by the right rear window, next to a young man who had a dog on his lap. The dog was about half the size of Xena and seemed well-behaved but squirmed a lot. This fellow, Drew, also had a pet rat in a cage at his feet. On his left was Jimmy who was headed back to Midland Texas to rejoin his pregnant wife. Up front with Eric was another guy, Gabe. As we introduced ourselves (which people who are going to have to be stuck with each other for an extended time are obliged to do), I realized that I was twice the age of even the driver and three times that of the others. The age difference seemed less important to all of us after they learned that Xena and I had just walked across the country and that I had even been to Woodstock. They realized that I wasn't just some old transient, I guess, but that there was still some life left in me!

Off we went but it seemed like we'd never get out of urban California. We had to pick up the sixth young man somewhere in the area northeast of Los Angeles. This took us through a maze of semi-suburban roads. It left me feeling like I was on a Greyhound bus, dragging from one stop to another, in the company of friendly but strange human beings.

Finally we hit the urban superhighways and gradually they turned into the regular old interstate; before long we were in Arizona. Every few hours we would stop for gas and to stretch our legs. Two or three of us would lift Xena, cage and all, out of the back. I'd take her for a quick walk, get her back in her cage and we'd stuff it back among the packs, nestled close up to the rear window of the cab. I'd grab an ice-cream bar or a soda and we'd be off again.

We stopped at a rest area that night for about four or five hours of sleep. As the old man, I got to stretch out on the back seat of the truck. Four guys went out and slept right on the ground and one guy took the front seat.

The next day we pulled off to rest in New Mexico and ran into two guys whose semi had broken down and who were waiting for a part. It happened that they were going right through the town where Drew (the guy with the dog and rat) was headed. At first, these two, Dennis and Turtle, weren't too keen on taking a rider, mainly because they already had a dog. They feared dog fights. But these guys were a lot like us, and after a good deal of chumming up and reconsidering, they took a what-the-heck attitude and said Drew could ride with them as soon as the part got there. I was ecstatic that I wouldn't have a dog on the lap to my left, but the rearrangement ended up with three of us again in the back. Off we went, slightly less crowded, making our way into and across Texas.

Before we would get to San Antonio, we had another guy to drop off. This was Jimmy, the one with the pregnant wife. He had to get to Midland, Texas. There is no way to go straight to San Antonio by way of Midland! It was at least three hours' drive out of our way. I checked the route and saw that it was actually a little shorter to go through Midland rather than first going to San Antonio. And Jimmy then informed us that not only was his wife pregnant, she was due any moment! When we dropped him off, his hugely pregnant young wife came out to greet us and we were all happy he had made it in time. We wished them a happy parenthood and took off for San Antonio.

I was so exhausted that I'm not sure, but I think we had to go through Dallas and then south for three more hours to San Antonio. At every stop we lifted Xena in and out and we never dropped her, a considerable accomplishment for a couple of tired guys lifting the shifting weight of a standing dog in a plastic carrier.

Eric dropped me off in San Antonio, and my niece and nephew, good ol' Becca and Nathan, came and got me and took me back to their sweet little home. Xena took off into the backyard. The kids crowded around. I had family again.

I looked out in the backyard at my van, still parked where I had left it three months before. I realized that finally the walk was truly over, I was essentially "home." Xena and I were both okay. We were not just "okay," we were stronger, smarter and more confident than ever before.

I knew then that I would have to begin sharing my experience with old friends and relatives, that I'd have to keep in touch now with many new friends, and that I'd have to reach out, to some extent, to anyone else who was interested. To do that, I'd have to write a book.

Postscript

Blog entry April 7: *Xena and I really struggled to get across the country and always part of our intent was to generate understanding and some financial support for Audubon. So if you can, send something for the birds. Thanks. I'm so grateful for so many new friends and old friends and for my wonderful family. I will hold all of you in my heart as long as I live.*

I'm sure the reader has noticed how my walk was full of people: people in cars, at convenience stores, running out from their homes, and even opening up their homes to me. They were my string of pearls, my safety net, my cure for loneliness. Without these people I met, the physical walk would have been rather barren, full of beautiful terrain but empty of human kindness. As it was, it was a rich and powerful experience carrying me along on some sort of wave from one improbable situation through another and on to yet another. The people I met were like guides along a trail. Most nights I hid from them, but by day I would dive right in again, trying to catch that inexplicable wave of human compassion.

People have asked me what I learned from making this walk. If you've read this book, you've experienced some of what I experienced, and therefore you've learned some of what I learned. I believe people should set their personal goals so high that it's not clear whether those goals are even reachable. Then after striving as hard as possible, it doesn't matter whether the entire goal has been reached. It only matters whether you've given your all. One way or another, you'll have found out what you're capable of accomplishing.

I made it to San Diego. That was enough for me. I won't become (I don't think) a habitual walker, but I do know more about myself. My persistence and my on-again-off-again bravery surprised me. I seem to have a renewed sense of confidence.

In the past, I've been able to achieve some of my goals, whether in Scouting, in travelling with my family, or in our theater group in Arkansas. But I think that none of those goals were as obviously difficult and unusual as was the attempt of this walk across America. In succeeding, I proved to myself that physically, mentally and socially, I could make it happen. If I had to be strong, I would push. If I had to be smart, I would think. And when I met new people, I would be warm, compassionate and truthful.

I don't remember being angry during the walk. Maybe I was angry at the wind in New Mexico, but certainly I wasn't angry at any people. When your heart and legs are faced with a constant need to push onward, it's really a waste of time being angry at obstacles of any kind.

I learned how to get by with little money and few comforts. I felt closer to nature, to the animals, and to the landscape. I felt closer to people than ever before. I found that it was good for me to be dependent on others.

The word "confidence" comes from the Latin word for "trust." I learned to trust others, to trust my surroundings, and to trust myself. Trust implies taking a risk. If you lend someone money, you trust them to pay you back; that's a risk you take. As I go into my later years now, I know I'll be even more willing to take risks, to live in a state of excitement, trusting that living that way will mean that whatever happens will be better than if I were just watching my life fly to its end from some safe corner.

What's next? I'll start out again, not on the road this time, but on the track of some other things I want to do and to write. I've always wanted to canoe the Mississippi River from its source up in Minnesota. Anyone want to do that? Get in touch! Of course Xena rides in the middle. No dog paddling.

A person's life is so much more than any one accomplishment. Maybe Neil Armstrong would like to be remembered for what a great chess player he was or whatever, and maybe Shakespeare would have liked to be recalled as a dedicated grandfather. We're all so complex.

My grandchildren will probably remember me as the granddad who walked across America. That's cool, but I hope they remember me as well for the work I did with the theater and for how much I loved being a dad and a granddad. Some religions believe that our souls have to hang around in the afterlife until no one mentions our name ever again. Those souls can only then move on to something better. My walk may have extended my time in purgatory, but I have to say it was well worth it.

A great horned owl in Alabama.

Appendix A: The Bird List

Blog entry September 16: *It's hot. I'm at a convenience store, near Alma, GA. We're only able to walk 'til about 11 o'clock in the morning. I wish that I could do more birding. But the time of year being summer, there are just the regular summer birds; like I saw a Summer Tanager yesterday and I heard Barred Owls last night. I don't know if I mentioned seeing the Wood Stork the first day out, back down around the coast. That that was nice to see a Wood Stork. But I haven't been able to do much birding. Also because I have to start early in the morning to use the cool hours of the morning. [At these times, I have to keep walking, so I can't actively bird.]*

These are the 165 bird species I recorded on the walk. (Note to serious birders: No rarities here, sorry! But I did see the Tropical Mockingbird that had been spotted at Sabine Woods on the East Texas coast as I was driving back from San Antonio! A first North American record bird!!)

Cardinal
Carolina Wren
Carolina Chickadee
Tufted Titmouse
Blue-Gray Gnatcatcher
Brown Thrasher
Mockingbird
Northern Parula
Black and White Warbler

Eastern Towhee
Red-Bellied Woodpecker
Turkey Vulture
Bald Eagle
Summer Tanager
Red-Tailed Hawk
Red-Shouldered Hawk
Clapper Rail
Wood Stork
Great Blue Heron
Great Egret
Snowy Egret
Cattle Egret
Tri-Colored Heron
Blue Jay
Fish Crow
American Crow
Boat-Tailed Grackle
White-Eyed Vireo
Laughing Gull
Ring-Billed Gull
Rock Pigeon
Pileated Woodpecker
Black Vulture
Mourning Dove
Common Ground Dove
Loggerhead Shrike
Barred Owl
Eastern Screech Owl
Eastern Bluebird
House Sparrow

Canada Goose
Mallard
Blue-Winged Teal
Whippoorwill
Starling
Chimney Swift
Eurasian Collared Dove
Barn Swallow
Tree Swallow
Cat Bird
Brown-Headed Cowbird
Ruby-Throated Hummingbird
Killdeer
Broad-Winged Hawk
Downy Woodpecker
Indigo Bunting
Great Horned Owl
Savannah Sparrow
Eastern Meadowlark
American Kestrel
Chuck-Will's-Widow (Huh? Weird name for a bird... -Lucy)
Brown-Headed Nuthatch
Chipping Sparrow
Belted Kingfisher
Sanderling
Dunlin
Royal Tern
Brown Pelican
Willet
Merlin
American Coot

Northern Shoveler
Gadwall
Ring-Necked Duck
Red-Winged Blackbird
Palm Warbler
Sandhill Crane
House Wren
White Ibis
Black-Necked Stilt
Short-Billed Dowitcher
Lesser Yellow Legs
Greater Yellow Legs
Least Sandpiper
Snipe (Wait, are these real? -Lucy)
American Pipit
Glossy Ibis
Black-Bellied Plover
Marsh Wren
Ruby-Crowned Kinglet
Swamp Sparrow
Virginia Rail
Yellow-Rumped Warbler
Black-Bellied Whistling Duck
Lesser Scaup
Pied-Billed Grebe
Ruddy Duck
Northern Pintail
Black Skimmer
White Pelican
Semi-Palmated Sandpiper
Ruddy Turnstone

Forster's Tern
Little Blue Heron
Anhinga
Hooded Merganser
Robin
Bobwhite
Song Sparrow
Field Sparrow
Neotropic Cormorant
Snow Goose
White-Fronted Goose
Long-Billed Curlew
Vermillion Flycatcher
Western Kingbird
Double-Crested Cormorant
Cooper's Hawk
Barn Owl
Ross' Goose
Cinnamon Teal
Black Crowned Night Heron
Green Kingfisher
Ringed Kingfisher
Kiskadee
Raven
Golden Fronted Woodpecker
White Winged Dove
Roadrunner
Sage Thrasher
Canyon Towhee
Black Throated Sparrow
Cactus Wren

Say's Phoebe
Black Phoebe
Lark Bunting
Western Meadow Lark
Brewer's Sparrow
Brewer's Black Bird
Prairie Falcon
Phainopepla
Vesper Sparrow
Curve Billed Thrasher
Ash-Throated Fly Catcher
Black-Chinned Hummingbird

Note: I was feeling like I hadn't seen that many birds on my walk. Then I heard from Florrie Lennon, a friend in Pennsylvania, who said, "Wow! I didn't know there even *were* that many different birds!"

Appendix B: The "Unintelligible" Blog

Throughout my walk, I was able to communicate by blogging, thanks to new voice-recognition technology and to my sister-in-law Jean, and my daughter, Lucy. I was able simply to phone Jean and leave my blog as a message for her. She had an App which would translate my verbal message into print automatically. She would then email those words to Lucy, who would edit out small errors and post my blog verbatim on our website. This process saved me, a veritable techno-dinosaur, from slowly typing on my tiny cell phone; I couldn't have been happier or more grateful.

It wasn't until I returned from San Antonio to Pittsburgh that I learned from Lucy that the printed text she received was often fraught with errors and that the editing process had sometimes been challenging and quite puzzling. (She had instructed me to speak as clearly and slowly as possible to minimize this problem.)

I learned the extent of this through an error Lucy had made on my Christmastime blog. Lucy had gone through and made her corrections and, as always, had saved the original in case she needed to recheck my "original" words. She always posted her corrected version on the website, but this time, she accidentally posted the original exactly as it had been received. In Pittsburgh, she showed me what had been posted and it was hilarious. I can only imagine what the readers of my blog must have thought: that I was either drunk or had broken down under the freezing Texas rains. This is the unedited version that appeared on the website. I share it with you as a tribute to Lucy's dedication to her efforts for me.

The "Unintelligible" Blog: *Hello Hello everybody, sorry I haven't logged for a while. Sometimes between visiting people and just been kinda tired sometimes. I just don't do it is office I should. But anyway, here's a new update. I'm almost in Houston, so I'm looking forward to that. Hey, I didn't tell you about the signs coming in to Texas. Whenever you come in to Texas. The sign says your friendly the Texas way bye that refers to is the fact that the Ballroom on the side of the road is paved and wide enough for a car on both sides, meaning. People can get over. If someone wants to get by. Hey vendors is beautiful dance with the Texas drivers do, which reduces road rage in because you don't have stock behind people as much. It also means that maybe walking along the burned haven't gone to be wary of people moving over to let somebody pass. Yes I enjoyed visiting. What is Chad and Amber. Williams in Louisville. When I first off to Texas. That was a very cold night and I had a great time sleeping in their shed and having some breakfast with them in the morning We're, great family and Sabine, Lamar hosted me for 2 nights, your couch surfers yeah and Beaumont. And it was great visiting with her the next day. Christine slave yeah spelled S L I V A. By the way took me out. Boating for about 8 hours. We had a great time. Call lot over. Probably 100 or more red tail hawk. 4 million fly. Katrina Western King bird at the end of the day. Yeah it was great. Yeah, I really enjoyed it. Yo my routine. I decided I will tell you a little bit about my routine. Because it's gotten to be well, very routine. Part 1 Yes, I bye. Yeah I'm walking about 12 miles a day and, I tried to spaces. So I get to work town, with at least a convenience store, during the day, the error I get my supplies such as in ice cream sandwich and a coke zero. I know, I know plenty of water And I head out of town, until I can find a place, by about 430 in the woods your OH area. Yeah rack.*

Appendix C: The Casa Grande Dispatch Article

In the chapter on Arizona, I mentioned that Bill Coates of the Casa Grande Dispatch had written a special article about our walk. I always hoped I'd be able to include it in this book. Used with the newspaper's kind permission, here it is:

Taking the dog out for a long, long walk

By Bill Coates
Valley Life Editor
March 22, 2012

Brad Storey walked to the March 5 meeting of the Tucson Audubon Society.

"I made it just in time," he said.

If he had been a few minutes late, the members would have understood. After all, it was a long walk. Storey had started out from the Georgia coast some six months before. By the time he reached Tucson, he wanted to stop at the Audubon Society to tell the gathering how things were going.

His walk across America is a fundraiser for Audubon and birds. It's a natural cause for a serious birder like Storey.

When he meets people, he says, "I just give them my card and tell them what I'm doing. I'm raising money for bird habitat."

He pushes a cart filled with water and supplies and sporting a banner that reads: "Coast to Coast for Audubon."

Storey, 66, talked about his long walk as he sat in the patio of Casa Grande artist Campbell Auer. Storey was well-tanned, as you might expect from a couple thousand miles of open air.

He was trim, having lost some 20 pounds since starting out. His beard hinted that shaving wasn't high on his list. He was a long way from his hometown, Mena, Ark.

Auer and Storey met some 12 years ago, when Storey came through Casa Grande on a birding trip. His van needed repair so he made his way to a paint store. A house painter by trade, Storey thought it a good place to ask if anybody needed an extra hand. Auer came in to buy paint. The two struck up a dialogue and Storey landed some house-painting work at Auer's place. They kept in touch. So when Storey was near Casa Grande late last week, he called Auer on his cellphone and got an invitation to stop by. Now in Auer's backyard, Storey rested his tired "dogs"—and his dog. As it turned out, it wasn't simply a long walk for birds. It was a long walk with a 3-year-old Siberian husky named Xena.

Their walk began on the shores of the Atlantic Ocean. It was Sept. 7. He had told his children, all grown, of his plans. He had talked the talk. Now he had to walk the walk.

"I started out on Jekyll Island on the Georgia coast—one foot in the water, one foot facing west."

He didn't see his odds as all that great, at first.

"I never thought I'd get across Georgia."

Once he cleared Georgia, he figured he might have a shot. He soon became tuned into the cadence and culture of walking the highways and byways and finding food and board. He hit the convenience stores for water, ice cream sandwiches, Swiss cheese and Andes Mint Cookies. He slept wherever he felt comfortable setting up his tent. For that reason, he liked hiking along railroad tracks. Trees or bushes were often planted as a buffer from nearby roads. They offered good cover. Xena offered good protection.

"I could not have made this trip without her, both for companionship and for safety," Storey said.

Safety also dictated some ground rules. Storey generally followed them, though not always. For one thing, he didn't sleep under bridges, though he did once in Texas—quickly learning why he came up with the rule in the first place. He and Xena were joined by three or four men he suspected were illegal immigrants, hiding out and waiting for a ride. They asked Storey if he'd share the space so they could spend the night. He could hardly say no.

They seemed nice enough. Still, he wasn't sure they wouldn't murder him in his sleep. He didn't have to worry, though. Their ride soon arrived and man and dog got a peaceful night's rest.

Another rule was he didn't accept rides. But he made an exception to that, too, once again in Texas, as he found himself unable to make any headway against gale-force winds. A woman pulled up and asked if he was Brad Storey.

She recognized him from the Internet website, CouchSurfing. It matches travelers with hosts that provide free lodging for a night. Storey had registered with the site.

He recalled spending the night with a nice hippie couple in Mississippi.

"They had lava lamps in the bathroom."

The woman in Texas offered him a ride. At first he refused but changed his mind after she told him winds were expected to top 60 mph. Storey met a lot of nice people like her. Many would stop and ask him how he was doing.

"As individuals, people are wonderful people," he said. In groups, it's a different story. In groups, people take sides and aren't on their best behavior.

One group ranks high in Storey's book, though. Railroad engineers. Outside Sanderson, Texas, a Union Pacific engineer who happened to be driving down the highway spotted Storey wearing an orange Union Pacific ball cap. Storey had found it hanging from a tree near the tracks. The engineer stopped to chat. He and his wife later booked a motel room for Storey in Sanderson. He also told his Union Pacific colleagues about Storey. Now they know him by his dog and his orange cap as they pass him on the rails.

"They toot me," Storey said.

Train toots apparently don't bother Xena. She's a good traveler and well-behaved, Storey said, though, she does strain at the leash when she sees something worth chasing or getting acquainted with.

"She loves squirrels, dogs, cats, pigs—well, not pigs—we've seen javelina," Storey said.

He left Auer's on Tuesday, having waited for the wintry storm to pass.

He expects to finish up in San Diego, where he'll likely do more than dip his toe in the Pacific.

"I'm probably going to fall in face first," Storey said.

He still has to cross large stretches of desert to get there. He got the cart in Texas, in part, to carry the water he's going to need. Another coast-to-coast walker he met told him which kind of cart to get. Good advice. He also told Storey it was OK to walk on Arizona interstates. Bad advice. A Highway Patrol officer stopped Storey in his paces on Interstate 10 outside Tucson. Wheels were allowed. Feet weren't. The officer called Storey a cab, which he and Xena took to the nearest frontage road.

From there, it was just a short walk to an Audubon meeting.

Appendix D: The Most Asked Questions and "Fun Facts"

1. What made you want to do something like this?
2. How many pairs of shoes did you go through?
3. Do you ever think of quitting?
4. Where do you sleep at night?
5. Do you have everything you need?
6. What do you do in the rain? What do you eat? How do you stay clean?
7. Did you see any new birds?
8. Has anyone been bad to you?
9. Have you been scared?
10. What will you do when you get there?
11. Do you want to sell that dog?
12. Is it a thrill? (Only asked once.)
13. Are you going to write a book?
14. What's next?

I heard all of these questions many times. People asked me about these things because they were interested in my trip and were curious; but there was usually also a deeper reason: they were concerned for me. I suppose that going even deeper, they imagined themselves in my shoes (appropriately) and wondered how they might fare in the same situation. I tried to answer each person sincerely. I knew I was speaking from a different podium than in my normal life. My questioner was seeing me as a representative of some almost alien life form sometimes, doing something they could not see themselves doing.

First of all, no one treated me badly—not one person!

I told those who asked, that I was often scared, especially when I would first get in my tent at night. I never knew if I was completely safe from the view of the road. I felt quite vulnerable. I told people that I often thought of quitting, but as the title of this book indicates, I couldn't take that option. I told everyone that not a single person had given me a hard time. I was not seen as a transient, a drifter, but rather as a man with a purpose. I had not come to their town or their county to take advantage of anything or anyone. I think most people saw me as someone interesting, with an interesting dog, passing through on an interesting mission.

People called to me from their cars, came up to me as I sat on the cement outside convenience stores, and offered me best wishes in the form of water bottles, dog food, places to camp and beds in which to sleep.

In the rain I tried to stay dry but I got wet too often. Luckily I didn't see much rain! I ate a lot of Swiss cheese and Andes Mints and any chocolate I could get, Subway sandwiches, cheese crackers, ice-cream sandwiches and Coke Zeros. (My diet was actually terrible!) I didn't stay as clean as I would have liked, but there were creeks in the East and always there were bathrooms in the convenience stores and Subways which often had a lock so I could "freshen up" in private.

What made me want to walk across the country? I told folks that I had always wanted to do something on a grand scale. I knew I couldn't climb Mount Everest, but I thought that with persistence, I might make it across America. I told people that I camped out along the road, behind bushes and trees, away from the town limits, and that I never crossed fences or went past "No Trespassing" signs. When asked if I needed anything, I'd usually say no, unless it was late in the day, and then I'd ask about a place to camp. I think people were always impressed or at least curious, that I didn't ask for money or food. They could see right away that I wasn't panhandling. That was good. It put us on an equal footing. My new friends and I were then able to reach out to one another with mutual generosity.

Shoes? I went through a pair about every 400 miles, six pairs in all. Birds? I enjoyed telling people about the bird life I had seen, but my trip only allowed for a few visits to special bird areas. I didn't see any species I'd never seen before, but I did see and list about 165 different species (see Appendix A). When asked (often) what I would do when I got to the Pacific, all I could say was that I honestly didn't know, that that concern was going to be part of the mystery of my walk, just like the end of my life will remain a mystery to me until I get there! I guess they could tell that I wasn't too worried. You know, "sparrows of the field" and all.

Often I was asked if I'd sell Xena. I told one young man that I'd have to have a half-million dollars for her. His eyes widened and he said, "Really? That much?" I couldn't believe he thought I was serious and I quickly assured him I was kidding, and that I'd never part with her. For a moment though, he had thought that he was looking at a dog worth a cool half-million bucks!

Was it a thrill? Yes, definitely. Now, much of the walk was a struggle; however, struggle has its own component of thrill unless we get wrapped up in pitying ourselves for having to go through it. The joys that came along were enjoyed so much more, as long as the lows hadn't brought me down too much.

And yes, I'm going to write a book. If I don't, I might forget what we did and I can't count on Xena to remind me of anything! All she wants to know, similar to that last question, is "What now?"

Fun Facts

Length of Trip: 2,556 Miles (approximately)

Time of Trip: 167 Days Walking, 135 Nights Spent in the Tent

Overall Time Span: Seven Months
(September 7, 2011 to April 6, 2012)

Weight of Backpack: Varied Between 35 and 45 Pounds
(Eastern Half), Much Lighter in the West

Cart Type: Schwinn Bicycle Trailer (Converts to Stroller) With
Added Solid Core Tire Inserts, Reinforced Handle and
Modified Front Wheel

Miles Per Day: Averaged 12 First Half, 18 Second Half,
26 miles maximum in a day

Speed: Three Miles Per Hour,
Usually Five to Nine Hours Per Day

Weight Lost: 28 Pounds

Gear and Supplies Carried: REI Quarter Dome Tent (T 1),
Self-Inflating 4-foot by 20-inch by 1-inch Sleeping Pad,
Medium Duty Sleeping Bag, Large Back Pack, Front Pack,
Front Fanny Pack, Camera, Cell Phone and Charger, Long
Pants, Polyester Athletic Shirts, Rain Poncho, Thermal

Underwear, Thermal Overshirt, Winter Coat with Hood, Knit Hat, Ski Mask, Gloves, Ball Cap, Notebook and Pens, Small Coil of Rope, Dog Bowl, Three-Pound Bag of Dog Food, Three Gallons of Water in Cart (in West); and in Xena's "Outward Hound" Pet-Smart Pack, a First Aid Kit and Hygiene Supplies, Matches, Compass, and Flashlight

Cost of Trip: Practically Nothing, Just Food and 10 Motels, Probably about $15/Day average

Money Raised for Audubon: Approx. $2,500

Final Note: I recently discovered Leonard Cohen. How I missed him all my life, I can't explain. Here I will end the text portion of my book with this poem of his:

> *The road is too long*
> *the sky is too vast*
> *the wandering heart*
> *is homeless at last*

Through the
Looking Glass

Starting out at Jekyll Island, Georgia.

The bridge in Georgia where I left my worn-out shoes.

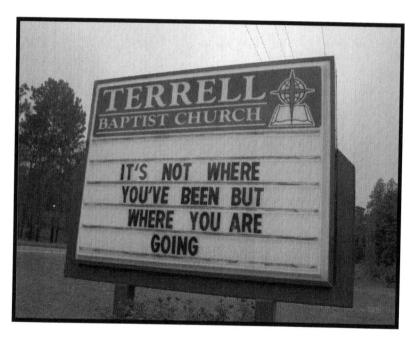

An ironic sign in Terrell County, Georgia.

Meeting members of an Audubon chapter
near Meridian, Mississippi.

The carved "Angel Tree" in Bay St. Louis, Mississippi, where Hurricane Katrina survivors clung for their lives.

Xena and new friend at a Louisiana Wal-Mart.

Cypress trees in a Louisiana bayou.

On the road to Del Rio.

The river walk in Del Rio, Texas.
(Swimming in January!)

Me, my dog, my cart, and my Union Pacific hat.

My egg-womb in Marathon, Texas.

There is, however, a library!

Canine and equine encounter in Arizona.

This is typical of our campsites in the West.

A sentry in a barren landscape.

A few rare trees in Arizona.

The Montanez family, near Gila Bend, Arizona.
That's Misaella in the middle.

A salt-cedar refuge near Hyder, Arizona.

This store in Hyder, Arizona, is the only commercial source of food or supplies for 30 miles in any direction.

Relics dot the landscape of the West.

A makeshift spot of shade for a four- or five-hour respite from the heat in the California desert.

Six feet wet in the Pacific. Ocean Beach, California.

Made in the USA
San Bernardino, CA
20 June 2017